THE SYSTEM

Herr Schlegel

To my Son
Dale Slagley
and Nancy
Herr Schlegel
(Doug)

ATHENA PRESS
LONDON

THE SYSTEM
Copyright © Herr Schlegel 2003

All Rights Reserved

ISBN 1 931456 98 4

First Published 2003 by
ATHENA PRESS
Queen's House, 2 Holly Road
Twickenham TW1 4EG
United Kingdom

Printed for Athena Press

THE SYSTEM

About the Author

The author uses his family name of "Herr Schlegel" for his writings.

He was raised in a rural area of the Midwest, served four years in the navy and eight years in the naval air reserve. Most of his time he flew as an aircrewman in anti-submarine and training helicopters and fixed wing aircraft, and in transport-type aircraft. He graduated from Parks College of St. Louis University with a B.S. degree in aircraft maintenance engineering, and received an MBA from Webster University. He was employed by the federal government for over twenty-five years as an equipment specialist, and later as an aerospace engineer, reaching the executive level of management and supervisory responsibility. He is highly trained and experienced in project management, maintenance management, logistics management, international logistics, and test and evaluation management. For several years, he was a manager of testing aircraft and helicopters, electrical and mechanical subsystems, electronic warfare systems and advanced electronic countermeasures systems and subsystems.

He has had a FAA aircraft and power plant license. He is a licensed quality engineer (CA) and a past president of his State Society of Professional Engineers, also serving on national committees. He has received many awards, including Federal Engineer of the Year, State Government Engineer of the Year. For nine years he was a corporate president, receiving awards for quality and management, including Who's Who Worldwide for three years and a lifetime membership in Who's Who Worldwide, reserved for the top 30,000 business managers and leaders worldwide.

He is a life member of the VFW and active in the American Legion, Elks, Moose, and Civitans.

Contents

Introduction

A system is defined as a set or arrangement of things so related or connected as to form a unity or organic whole. We may compare this with a chain. It is a basic and simple system, connected by several links. We all know that a chain is only as strong as its weakest link. This is true of systems from the smallest to the largest systems, such as aviation and space. This concept can also be applied to everything we encounter in everyday, social, political, economical government, business, and industry, just to name a few. The strength of the chain will not usually be a perfect ten, nor fall below five, and will change frequently as some elements improve and some get worse. This is true in all areas of our system, including social, political, economical, government, business, and industry, just to name a few. Here we will address some of the elements that make up the system under which we live, and that affect our everyday life.

During the past several years, we have seen the deterioration of morals, etiquette, honesty, discipline, and mutual respect, just to name a few, that impact on our system. It has been related in numerous news media that the tenet of today's society is that it is okay to lie, cheat, steal, or anything possible to achieve a purpose, whether it is legal, moral, or ethical. This is evident in many businesses, government agencies, and some parts of our military forces. The chapter on Management Subversion outlines some of the methods used. We also include a sampling of experiences in business and government ethics violations.

We are in an era where people do not trust the government bureaucracy, whether it is local, state, national or international. A large percentage are worried about their future, retirement, health insurance, security, education, and moral and ethical issues. However, we cannot criticize the brave members who have the ability to volunteer and swing into action in an emergency. These are unequalled and respected around the Earth, despite the fact that some "manufacture" minutiae to justify their position.

The quality of many of the items we purchase has deteriorated, due to cost cutting and lack of experienced and loyal employees. Quality is usually the first to go, and experienced quality personnel are the first to go. This happened years ago in NASA, which led to the explosion on the launch platform of a space project, and loss of an entire crew. Some of the most experienced personnel are "railroaded" out and replaced with personnel with little or no education and experience, because they can be hired at a cheaper wage with fewer fringe benefits. The attitude of many manufacturers is "just get it out of the door", and let the customer worry about it. Many managers are hired/promoted because they are top sales people or technicians, but they often lack the education, skills, and the "backbone" to protect the customer and their dealers.

Our education system has deleted some of the subjects relating to morals, ethics, civics, history, psychology, philosophy courses, and there are subjects like sports, music, and others relating to the arts being considered for reduction or termination, mainly due to funding limitations. In some schools the student and/or teachers must provide their own supplies, including soap, paper towels, toilet paper, and other standard supplies. The lack of disciplinary power of teachers and administrators, the lack of family discipline, and parental neglect have resulted in serious problems in many schools. Good teachers are seeking other careers due to student problems, heavy record and report workload, and inadequate pay.

Our judicial and legal system is near disaster. The courts are so bogged down in criminal cases that they cannot handle civil cases in reasonable time. Our jails and prisons are overcrowded. The good attorneys do very well, but the majority are evidently not capable of putting a difficult case together, and do not seem to be trained to handle their caseload efficiently. The media recently reported that 25 percent of all attorneys are actively seeking another career. Many judges have been failures or just don't like the law, and escape into government to work as judges, with little courtroom experience. Several reports have been received of judges taking "payoffs" through trial attorneys for their clients.

Most attorneys charge exorbitant fees, as compared to other professions.

Our government was based on the Constitution and Bill Of Rights. These principles are violated every day. The principle of "a country of the people, by the people, and for the people" is past history. Facts are twisted out of proportion to the extent that moral and ethical principles are lost. Most government levels think that the average citizen is not capable of managing their own affairs, and that they must dictate what they must do, and when. The truth is that the average person is far more capable than government to handle their own affairs. The media has been full of moral and ethical violations by some of our leaders. During the 1990s the morals of our country have deteriorated, and our reputation worldwide. Leaders who are supposed to be role models are not fulfilling this role.

Our military forces have decreased badly. A decreasing number of veterans in the Congress and Senate has seriously degraded our readiness. Many military leaders will not admit this for fear of disciplinary action. The last ten years of poor leadership have caused our military to be seriously affected in manpower, and equipment.

We have experienced the most rapid growth in technology in history, which has caused advancements in communications, electronics, computer, space, and their applications. However, these have paved the way for fraud, and related activities. These, along with the near real time news reports have changed our lives forever.

These and other elements contained herein, including reasons, causes and possible solutions are outlined in the following chapters, together with a historical perspective, and where we stand today.

The terrorist attacks on New York and the Pentagon on September 11, 2001, were the worst disaster in the history of the U.S. No one will ever know how it could have been averted. The effects of that have had a serious impact on all aspects of our society, which has a domino effect on our system.

The purpose of this document is to create an awareness, and stimulate the reader to think about how we can make the twenty-first century better. It is not the intent to criticize any individual or entity.

The weaknesses in some elements are caused by people, and can only be changed by people. Some refer to these weaknesses as "a sign of the times", not realizing that they are correctable only through actions by people.

We hear about high salaries among news and sports personnel. Just remember, that in the end, we all pay for them.

Chapter I

BUSINESS AND MANUFACTURING

Business ethics, in general, have become a thing of the past. Of course, many businesses and manufacturers have survived the changes, mainly due to their commitment to Quality and fairness and honesty to their customers. As has been said, one rotten apple can spoil the whole batch. Most small-town businesses survive because they must provide goods and services to their neighbors and friends, who would abandon them entirely if they were dishonest. Most small town manufacturers participate in community affairs, and are highly respected. It seems to change to "dog eat dog" if they are purchased by a foreign corporation or a domestic conglomerate. Small business employs 75 to 80 percent of the workers in the U.S. The large national and foreign corporations seem to have the most violations, probably due to their profit motive. Their pay or salary are based on the profit of the company, and the company stock price increase. Business has expanded so rapidly that they can't hire experienced and trained personnel, and some corporate executives are too overpaid.

An elderly retired bank president remarked that if you own a small business, you are the only one who is concerned whether your business is a success or whether is fails. The other associates, including co-owners, family (except maybe parents), suppliers, wholesale and retail lending institutions, city/local government, manufacturers, higher levels of government, friends, employees, and others, care less about your success or failure. They are in it for the benefit of themselves.

The old country's system of teaching the trades during high school, then an apprentice period before entering college seems to have worked well. This is probably why some of the most capable professional managers in our country were born and trained in Europe. One college professor commented several years ago:

"You engineers think that when you graduate you are going to be a 'hot-shot' engineer who knows everything. I have news for you. We give you the tools to learn with here. Your real learning starts when you begin your first job after graduation. Also, if your main goal is to make money, you are in the wrong place. If this is your main goal, you should be training for a truck driver, plumber, electrician, bricklayer or mason.

Dr. Demming was probably the world's expert on quality and productivity. He offered the American auto industry his ideas and methods for improvements in quality and productivity. They ridiculed him, told him they were doing alright, and didn't need his services. The Japanese auto industry hired him, and most of us saw what happened. They almost broke U.S. auto makers, and this is probably why we have so many foreign autos in this country today. The U.S. auto industry had to scramble feverishly to find some way to improve their quality and productivity. It appears that, overall, the U.S. makers have more recalls than the foreign made. Many recalls are not published, so if you have a problem, check with your dealer service manager. Some are covered even though your warranty has expired. This goes for anything, including appliances, and other items purchased.

Remember the Y2K scare at the beginning of the year 2000? Nothing happened, possibly because the retired programmers and designers were called in, because they designed the old programs, and were the only ones that could solve the problem. However, we must always be on the alert for scams and rip-offs. Beware of any "deals", and do not trust offers and do not open e-mail that you are unfamiliar with.

The manufacturing quality of products we use every day has continued to decline over the past several years. Contributing to the problems, or as some relate, adding to the problem, is the opening of free world trade, through NAFTA and others, causing companies to move their operations to other countries where they can get lower operating costs, and what is called "slave labor" at a fraction of U.S. labor costs. However, we haven't seen the retail costs lower. These companies are using the lower cost of production to increase profit and inflate the value of their stock. The Dow-Jones Average has been so inflated that many investors are hurt badly.

While prices have skyrocketed, it has become necessary for both husband and wife to work to maintain a medium standard of living. The percentages of bankruptcies has been rising every year. More families are using savings and inheritances to meet regular living expenses. Many wonder if this is due to necessity or the desire to live above their means. Also, some are refinancing their homes to pay off debts relating to basic living needs.

Years ago many workers worked for almost a lifetime at one place, did their job well and were satisfied. They retired in the community, and were productive for the rest of their lives. Their earnings went back into the local economy, and their retirement was large enough for a comfortable income. At present, most jobs are not permanent. Large companies now lay off older employees just before they are eligible to retire, with no benefits. There is an increasing number of single parents, which requires companies and schools to provide day care services. This may be the cause of some of the problems with teens in our society. The stress on workers causes premature strokes and other medical problems at an early age. Years ago we never heard of people in their twenties and thirties having heart attacks and strokes, as well as other disorders.

How many times have you tried to purchase a U.S. made product, and couldn't find one? It is getting more difficult every day. It is getting more common every day to learn of tainted fruits and vegetables, mostly produced and shipped from outside the United States. Cold cut meats that we used to eat and make sandwiches with are now dangerous to consume without re-cooking them. The practice of home canning and freezing will become more popular as problems increase. There is also an increase in families that purchase their meats from the producer or butcher, thereby greatly reducing the chance of strange bacteria, and coming in contact with other undesirables.

Have you noticed the increase in bottled water? There has been a tremendous increase in sales of bottled water. In some parts of the U.S., the mineral content is high, and correlates with the high incidence of gallstones and kidney stones. Calcium, of the insoluble type, seems to be the main culprit. Also, many of the additives in most urban water systems have an undesirable taste and may have some long-term effects on health. Basically calcium is essential to the human body, but it must be in a soluble form. Some alternatives to bottled water are water distillers, and water filtering systems and faucets. Personally I have used a water distiller for the past twelve years, and have had no indications of any stones. I have my distiller connected to a separate faucet, and it is connected to my refrigerator ice maker and water cooler. Thus all the water we consume, including drinking, cooking, and tea and coffee making is distilled, at a 99.8 purity level.

As mentioned previously, the American auto industry was forced to "clean up their act", due to the foreign influence. The next that faces dire consequences is the recreational vehicle industry. I have been involved in camping and recreational vehicles since the 1960s, during the years since, until about 1993, the dealers were honest, the manufacturers were trustworthy and cared for the dealers and customers. The retail customers were mostly honest, and as a group are still the most congenial that you will ever meet. As the demands were increasing, many corporate sales personnel decided to manufacture their own brand. Several produced anywhere from a few to one hundred, and due to lack of capitalization, went out of business, leaving the dealers and customers "high and dry" on warranty coverage. Recreational vehicles include motor homes, travel trailers, fifth wheels, fold down (commonly called pop-ups), and truck campers (commonly called slide-ins). Although there have been many advances in the manufacturing process, they have not solved the water leakage problem. As a matter of fact, it has been worse since 1994. Some companies, such as Jayco, Winnebago and Tiffin Motor Homes (Allegro), have kept their quality standards high. Travel Trailers, receiving good marks are Coachmen, Jayco, Holiday Rambler, etc. However, the industry as a whole has fallen victim to the increase in demand, difficulty in hiring qualified personnel, and consolidation of companies. The corporate attitude is to produce the units at the lowest cost, and let the dealers and customers correct the problems that should have been corrected prior to shipping to the dealer. For example, a company started in Goshen, IN, in 1988, produced a good product at a reasonable cost up to 1993. Then after being purchased by another company, quality deteriorated, they did not have any service center, and dealers and customers became disenchanted with the product. Of course the company blamed the dealer. Now, after being the no. 1 seller in 1993, they have slipped and lost several good dealers as well as retail customers. This was caused by lack of ability of management, sales personnel handling service problems, and dollar signs in the sales manager's eyes. Anyone interested can check Houston Co, AL Circuit Court Case CV95-444-L. One customer took his travel trailer to eight different dealers, and twice to the factory, for manufacturing defects. The manufacturer would not recall the unit nor replace it.

Many years ago, a college engineering professor remarked that in this country we were going to run out of experienced personnel to train the newcomers. This is evident today in any industry we deal with. Now, we have too many "smart alecs", who think they know more they know more than anyone, simply due to the position they occupy, not by experience.

Telemarketing has become very popular, especially telephone service, credit card providers, home mortgage companies, insurance companies, and other pure "scams". The Internet has become a "haven" for scam artists and computer hackers.

It is virtually impossible to hire honest, dependable personnel and contractors. The smaller, independent contractors are best, but we still need written contracts and a specified warranty on every job. One instance was reported where the architect specified one item the request for bids specified the same specifications, for an item we will call "manor". The landscape contractor, to make the lowest bid, and more profit, contracted with another supplier to build an item that looked identical, and the cost was less than half of the manor. However, the finish was less than half the thickness. The welded joints began to rust after three months on site. Other installations of the "manor" are in excellent condition after four to five years. More of this will be discussed in the government section.

Our government has pushed free trade and NAFTA for several years. Now U.S. companies are moving to Mexico and other countries. These products are not subject to import taxes and the labor rates are much lower. But watch the quality. This not only increases our trade deficit, but seriously affects our domestic employment and economy. I can see the day, not too far off, when we will be "bitten back" for our mistakes, foreign wages will increase, and prices will skyrocket, adding to the inflation woes. For example, the textile industry in the U.S. has lost two-thirds of its employment. The small town, under 15,000, has been hit the hardest mainly in the South. One county has recently increased in unemployment from 11 percent to 17 percent. Ask these people how good the economy is. In other words don't believe the figures the government releases. They are tailored to political advantage, and I believe they are inaccurate.

In general, quality has been ignored in the workplace, in government, and much of industry. Many of the problems today are due to administrators making decisions purely on economic and political influence. Thus engineering, especially quality engineering, have been ignored. Just take a look at the many recalls on everything from meats and vegetables and other food products, to automobiles, appliances, toys, etc. Disasters such as recent airline crashes and military accidents reflect serious quality problems. It appears, again, that non-engineers are making decisions they are not qualified for. Costs seem to override engineers' recommendations, resulting in some of these disasters, and caused by administrators not being trained nor cognizant of engineering principles.

How many times have you called a business and got a recording that they were not available, and to leave a message? This is getting more common as time goes on. Good common business practices dictate that if a business is open from 8:00 A.M. to 5:00 P.M., someone should be available to answer the phone. This is more important in small businesses, mainly having a sales goal. About 50 percent of people will not talk to an answering machine. If they want to buy an item, they will try someone who answers the phone.

However, it is becoming an idea of some businesses that if a customer wants to buy an item, they will leave a message or call back. Again, this is not true in about 50 percent of prospects. Thus sales are lost due to lack of attention on the part of the business.

More and more sales personnel are nothing but order takers. They do not circulate among prospects and develop business relationships among potential customers. As an old saying goes, get out there and search the bushes for business.

Another fallacy, similar to government purchasing activities, is the specification development. Many contractors write specifications for a particular project, using a previous purchase, and copy it almost verbatim. Also several government agencies, mostly city, county, and state, hire the contractor they want to get the contract, to develop the specification. Although most procedures call for competitive bidding, they circumvent the process to get the contractor they want. If they have a detailed specification for a particular item from a vendor, then it is unethical for other vendors to bid on the item, and this should be declared *sole source*. If the request for proposals is to be competitive, then the requirements should be broad, i.e., budget ceiling, functional requirements desired, and scope of what is to be included in the bid. This allows multiple vendors to submit their own specifications and performance characteristics for consideration.

As the economy gets tighter, and competition gets keener, the incidence of fraud, kickbacks, false/misleading advertising and claims, and other unprofessional and unethical activities is on the increase.

Chapter II

GOVERNMENT

Most government entities including city, county, state, federal, and international agencies are unaccountable for their actions. Larger government is full of self satisfaction and egotistical aims by individuals. The smaller communities elect well-known candidates who live in the local community, are usually well respected in their community, and are probably small business owners, as well as community leaders. If they "step out of line" they are immediately chastised by their peers.

The breaking point for cities is in the area of 20,000 to 30,000 population. After this, the politicians get greedy and pursue their own personal aims, many unknown to most residents. One city in southeast Alabama, with a population of around 70, 000, is a good example. How can a real estate broker spend $300,000.00 for a $60,000 job, finish out a three- or four-year term, and increase assets by in excess of one million? It is common for benefactors to donate to campaign costs, but who's fooling who? They naturally expect to get their money back through special favors. The city manager, city commission and Chamber of Commerce all bow to the demands of the mayor. The city services are not as responsive as some other cities, and about 80 percent of businesses are run by liars, cheats, and opportunists.

The City Police Department personnel work their "tails" off to clean the city of drug dealers, prostitutes, rapists, murderers, etc. They lock horns with the city council over arresting gamblers and other acts, and are told to lay off. The chief threatens to resign, and one councilman is forced to resign. Then when the incompetent lawyers and judges get through arguing over cases that make it to the court, some are set free with probation, or a slap on the hand. Most continue to be offenders after their release.

State governments have gone to uncaring for the average citizen and small business. Years ago, the attorney general of the state had a lot of clout, and would "lower the boom" on any entity that did wrong to a citizen or business. Now, the attorney general's office is only there to protect the political system, and is not supportive of business or the citizen. If you have a problem they tell you to hire a lawyer. This will be discussed in the section on the judiciary and legal system.

State representatives are not experienced in management, and argue for their pet projects and against their political adversaries purely on political differences instead of what is good for the public or the state. If you need personal or business assistance, they will give you the runaround. Alabama made national headlines during the opening session of the legislature, when the governor and lieutenant governor fought over control of the Senate. It came to the point that the lieutenant governor kept a "jar" under the podium because he was afraid he would lose control if he took time to go to the bathroom. This was a battle over whether the Republican lieutenant governor or the Democrat president pro-tem would preside over the Senate. This standoff continued for the complete term of the Senate—a complete waste of the taxpayers' money. Other state departments have the same problem.

Several associations state wide, such as the State BAR, the state Nursing Home Association, the Mobile Home Manufacturers/Dealers Associations are responsible for solving complaints against members. This is like letting the fox guard the chicken house. This creates an opening for fraud, conspiracy, conflict of interest, and violation of business ethics, to name but a few. There is no state government agency that has any power or responsibility for enforcement. The attorney general's office has no "backbone" or responsibility for the average citizen. All effort is to support special interests. For example, many companies/corporations moved to the South from the North over many years, to lower their cost of operation, including taxes. Now many are moving to Mexico and other countries where labor costs and taxes are much lower. Many politicians will blame NAFTA and GATT for the businesses exodus, but some of the blame should go to the state government for taxing the companies heavily. Some of these taxes are: corporate tax, franchise tax, and other taxes levied on business. Alabama for years taxed out of state corporations at twice the rate as in state entities. The case had to go to the U.S. Supreme Court to get it equalized out. Now the state is having to raise about 150,000,000 dollars to make up for the "rape" of out of state corporations. The Southern states are trying to recruit business, but more business is moving out. It is time for these governments to wake up.

Medicaid administered by the states is a joke. One in particular concerns an elderly lady in her eighties who had open heart surgery, and subsequently bleeding ulcers, and had to abandon housekeeping. Of course, Medicare/Medicaid would not pay anything toward assisted living costs. These were $975.00 per month. She was forced to sell her house on which she had borrowed against with a second mortgage. The mortgages totaled over $32,000.00, monthly payments totaled $412.00 per month, and other expenses made monthly costs to total $652.55 per month. Income from Social Security was $584.00, and the contract sale $363.30, for a total of $947.00 per month. Most of the difference of $294.00 was taken up with additional medicine and doctor costs that insurance would not pay. She had to borrow an additional amount of $19,200.00 from a relative over about two years in the assisted living facility. When her health deteriorated to the point that required professional nursing care. Medicaid was applied for, and she was admitted on December 30, 1994, with another loan from a relative of $2,646.54 for the first month's care which was supposed to be reimbursed by Medicare. Subsequently, Medicaid would not allow nursing home expenses because her name was on the contract sale of her house. The forced sale was about $10,000.00 less than the appraised value. The nursing home is presently suing the relative for $7,636.70.

The state Medicaid doesn't care about personal losses. They have not agreed to pay arrears to the nursing home. They continue to complain of lack of funds, but letters are sent to all persons attaining the age of sixty-five, advertising for participation. Also they want to expand coverage to children from these funds. In summary it appears that they have discriminated against some who have contributed greatly to the system, over people that have not and probably never contribute anything to the system. The norm for Medicaid is the people who have never had anything and have been on government support most of their lives. Many lawyers have gotten rich by suing the government over their mismanagement. Now Medicaid hires lawyers to find some way to cheat applicants when they are down and out.

California seems to lead all states in enforcing quality standards, followed by the northern and western states. Among the southeast, and south, Texas, Florida, and Georgia lead with the "Bible Belt" states of Alabama, Mississippi and Louisiana trailing the rest. The strength of attorney generals and secretaries of state seem to follow the same trend.

The federal government is the most distrustful. Forecasts and figures are designed to prove the goal of the releaser based on what is politically good. For the past eight years we had shame cast on the White House. The Oval Office was no longer an honor, but the scene of sex, lies, and deceit. The Lincoln bedroom has been used as a high-priced "hotel" for special guests of the president, to achieve political and/or financial gain. The mood of our country has improved considerably due to the change of politics in Washington, D.C., but we still will suffer many years for the damage by the previous administration.

Do you think social security can be relied on? Think again. The intent was good when it was implemented. It was a savior for many people. However, the system has not kept up with the cost of living, and at present it is only a meager supplement. Everyone now of working age cannot rely on social security and Medicare totally. All must have another retirement plan and a Medicare supplement plan for the major part of retirement.

For example if you work out a federal retirement, and then work in the private sector for ten years for social security, your social security benefits will be reduced up to one half. Also, half of these benefits are taxed for Income Tax purposes. In other words, you are double-taxed.

An attorney friend recently told me that you cannot sue a government agency. He has spent three years trying to get his uncle on Medicaid, and consequently broke four families. The government specifies a two-year limit on fraud, and requires many hours and cost on appeals.

Politicians have talked about saving social security for the past eight years. You may ask how can this be a problem in a civilized society. First, the federal bureaucrats have been "tapping" the Social Security Trust Fund to pay other expenses for the past twenty to twenty-four years. This is also most of the "surplus" we hear so much about.

The news has brought out that we are and have been getting 2 percent interest on the trust fund. This is another instance of mismanagement, because we should have been getting at least 4 percent, and maybe 5 or 6 percent. In order to generate more "surplus", many hospitals may be forced to close due to reductions in Medicare payments. At one time it was adequate for an elderly couple to live comfortably on social security. This is not the case now, because maximum social security benefits are about $15,000 per year. This is why both must work for a lifetime to achieve an adequate retirement. Also many of today's wage earners are already investing in stock options, 401 K, and other savings plans that employers sponsor and may pay part of the participation.

Here is another slant on social security that a correspondent came up with:

Our senators and congressmen do not pay into social security and, therefore do not collect from it. Social security benefits were not suitable for them. They felt they should have a special plan. The same goes for the Federal Employees' Retirement Plan. Many years ago they voted in their own plan. In recent years, no Congress person has felt the need to change it. After all it is a great plan. The only problem with it is maybe it should be a subject for Tom Brokaw's *Fleecing of America*. For all practical purposes, it works like this: when they retire, no matter how long they have been in office, they continue to draw the same pay until they die, except it may increase from time to time by cost of living adjustments. For example, former Senator Bradley and his wife may be expected to draw $7,900,000.00 over an average life span, with Mrs. Bradley drawing $275,000.00 during the last year of her life. Their cost for this is "0", nada, zilch. This little perk they voted in for themselves is free to them. You and I pick up the tab for this plan. Retirement plan funds come directly from the General Fund. Our tax dollars at work!

Social security, which you and I pay into every payday for our own retirement, with an equal amount matched by our employer, we can expect to get an average of $1,000.00 per month. Or, we would have to collect our benefits for sixty-eight years and one month to equal the Bradleys' benefits. Imagine, for a moment that you could structure a retirement plan so desirable, a retirement plan that worked so well, that railroad employees, postal workers, federal employees and others who were not in the plan would clamor to be included.

This is how good social security could be, if only one small change was made. That change would be to jerk the Golden Fleece Retirement plan out from under the senators and congressmen. Put them into the social security plan with the rest of us. Watch how fast they would fix it, and quit tapping the trust fund to pay other expenses. Social security and the education system will probably never be solved, because the politicians would not have a program to use in arguments These will continue to be weakened links in our *system*.

Another problem with government agencies lies within the procurement process. Specifications are written by employees with little experience in technical matters. Many look for a specification to copy, from a friend in the industrial community, or the manufacturer of the particular item that they desire to get the contract. Thus the manufacturer with a better reputation and/or better quality product doesn't stand a chance. This is why government has so many production problems, and hardware or software that they cannot use, or is substandard.

Chapter III

JUDICIAL AND LEGAL SYSTEM

Our judicial system as a whole is near disaster. It is alright for the very elite who can afford to advance through the court system until they can get a satisfactory decision, to the U.S. Supreme Court if necessary. However, most of us cannot afford to pay an attorney $100 to $300 per hour, plus expenses, to go that far. They are lucky to get through a circuit court, but the chances at this level are virtually non-existent for the plaintiff. In other words, we have no victim's rights.

There are several good attorneys who reach state attorney general, governor, senator and U.S. representative levels as small-town attorneys and judges. However, the norm is attorneys who cannot form an unbiased opinion do not know or can't interpret the law effectively. They rely on attorneys' pleas, so the attorney who presents the most effective side usually wins the case, regardless of the witnesses and proof that exists. The normal attorneys and judges are nine to five "ho-hum", non-aggressive types.

The 2000 election in Florida was an example. Both sides had the resources to go to the U.S. Supreme Court to get a final decision. There is no way to determine the voters thoughts by a "dimpled chad". In the first place this is 1970 technology but it is the best that the local election boards can afford. The answer, change to a modern optical scanner system or accept the percentage of spoiled ballots.

The following are examples of one Southeast Alabama circuit judge. The following article was taken from a local newspaper. The circuit judge isn't a member of the Swedish Bikini team, but he still made it into the January issue of *Playboy* magazine.

The men's magazine, which publishes photos of nude and scantily clad woman, featured an incident that occurred in his courtroom in June of 1997 in a section of the magazine titled "Newsfronts: Sentencing Follies".

Ever since he ordered court security officers to tape a defendant's mouth shut, news media across the country and overseas have told the tale. The incident occurred after he had sentenced the defendant to twenty years in prison for cocaine possession.

As the judge left the courtroom for lunch, the prisoner yelled from a holding cell and made lewd comments about him. After the remark the judge ordered him gagged and brought back into the courtroom. As he sat with duck tape wrapped around his head the judge changed his sentence to life in prison.

The prisoner appealed the conviction and the judge has since removed himself as the presiding judge. The case has been reassigned to another circuit judge.

Since the judge ordered the prisoner's mouth taped shut news accounts of the incident have been published in newspapers from as far away as Alaska and Germany, along with coverage by Court TV and a mention of the incident by radio commentator Rush Limbaugh.

The next article was published in the same newspaper: a circuit judge is shooting down his own court order on Wednesday which had allowed a convicted felon to possess firearms, contradicting federal laws.

The judge had signed the order on Tuesday, allowing the prisoner to own firearms even though he pleaded guilty of a class C felony—stalking his wife—on April 30. He also has a 1995 misdemeanor conviction for harassing communications because he threatened to kill his ex-wife, which also makes him ineligible to possess firearms.

The judge said he couldn't comment on the case since it is still pending, but after a talk with the County Sheriff's Department operations commander, he indicated he planned to rescind the order.

The order was written by the prisoner's attorney, as part of a plea agreement allowing him to plead guilty to the stalking charge in return for a five-year prison sentence. The judge placed him on probation for five years in lieu of the prison sentence.

The lawyer said his client wanted the order to possess guns as part of the plea agreement so he could still hunt with his son. The assistant district attorney said he did not agree to the order, although he approved of him pleading guilty to the stalking charge.

If the judge rescinded the firearms order, his guilty plea would be withdrawn and he would ask that the case go to trial. The assistant district attorney said he didn't want the defendant to be allowed to withdraw his plea.

The order allowing the defendant to hunt was essentially the integral part of the plea bargain his lawyer said. The defense attorney said, "We'll definitely go to trial on this."

If the judge didn't rescind the order, it would contradict federal laws stating that a convicted felon may not possess a firearm and a person convicted on a domestic violence charge may not possess a firearm.

The sheriff's operations commander said he didn't see any basis for any legal foundation for this order. You can't rewrite federal law in the local courts. If the defendant is caught in possession of any firearms, the weapons will be seized.

Another article in the same newspaper shows some other concerns: a local judge has recused himself from the re-sentencing request of a convicted drunken driver who wants his manslaughter sentences reduced.

The circuit judge won't reconsider the sentencing the defendant. He has served less than four years for the 1993 manslaughter conviction. He killed three people in a wreck on US Highway 84.

Records show a $500 campaign contribution to the circuit judge's 1994 election fund by the company owned by the defendant's father.

The judge could not comment on the case because it is pending.

The case now goes back to the last presiding judge. He will reassign the case based on a rotating list of judges used in instances of recusancy.

If the defendant's request is granted, he could go free within a year. His request is, in part, based on good behavior during his prison time.

The defendant's attorney said the judge had no choice but to step aside after the newspaper printed an article about the re-sentencing request and the campaign contribution.

The news story put it in the perspective that the defendant's lawyer said that he couldn't do anything but recuse himself. He didn't think (the contribution) would have affected the way he decided the case.

His lawyer said the judge avoided the appearance of impropriety by stepping down, so there would be no question in anyone's mind about a decision.

The defendant wants his three sentences to be served concurrently, which would allow him to serve fifteen years instead of the nineteen he received. He is now eligible for parole in August 2001, but could be released sooner if the re-sentencing request is granted.

This is not the first time the circuit judge has dealt with a legal matter involving the defendant's family.

Within a few months of winning the 1994 race the judge threw out a case filed by the defendant's family. They filed suit against Alabama Power's Farley Nuclear Plant for repairs to a crane they owned, which was damaged at the plant.

The circuit judge determined the case to be baseless, according to the contract. An appeals court overturned his ruling and the matter was settled out of court.

Regardless of who presides over the case, one of the leading opponents of the re-sentencing is the survivor of the collision that killed his parents and sister. He doesn't think the defendant is ready for a second chance right now, he needs to serve a little more time. This boy does not need to go free.

He and his family were driving in June of 1993 when the truck hit them in a head-on collision. He suffered permanent injuries from the accident.

The defendant's blood alcohol content tested at more than twice the legal limit for alcohol. He also had previous convictions for driving under the influence and possession of marijuana.

The county district attorney said he planned to protest the defendant's request for re-sentencing because his current sentence is too light.

Also, the same judge had Case CV95-444-L whereby a local businessman was forced out of business by Indiana and Florida corporations. This judge was reported to ignore the plaintiff's attorney, witnesses, and proof of interference, conspiracy, and fraud. Two local attorneys represented the defendants, and gave them summary judgments against the plaintiff. After about five years, the plaintiff was evidently "sold out" by all the attorneys and judges. Incidentally, these defendants' attorneys are members of the same local bar, and are drinking and social "buddies" at local functions. Some comments since have eluded to possible payoffs. The case was reported to cost one of the corporations over one million dollars, and the other over 250,000 dollars, while the plaintiff received less than 30,000 dollars, from which he had to pay some legal costs. Most attorneys (about 90 percent) will, and evidently are taught to, lie, cheat and steal to achieve the satisfaction of whoever pays them. When hiring most attorneys, they want their fees up front (which range from $100 per hour upward).

The last eight years of the U.S. presidency and the 2000 election have shown a degradation of honesty and ethical behavior. The U.S. has become a society where it is okay to lie under oath. Overlooking the already heavy workload of the courts for election vote appeals has become serious.

Some refer to some of the ballots in Florida as too complicated. On the other hand a newscaster reported on November 17, 2000, that the ballot was shown to a group of 3rd and 4th grade students, and they had no problems with them. This same balloting system has been used for many years in various parts of the country with no problem. It has always been a given that some ballots are spoiled and thrown out from the count, but some cannot accept this fact.

Judges are supposed to interpret the law, but laws are so complex that many can't do this, and rely on whichever attorney can present the best appeal.

Generally, the plaintiff (victim) has no rights under the present system. Thus, we are going to continually let people who should be locked up walk the streets.

Again, I have known some very professional attorneys, but the system is flawed by the majority. The legal profession for years has been the most hated profession. Lately, the banking profession has overtaken the attorneys as the number one hated profession. As one commented, he has more respect for prostitutes than attorneys in general.

One of the principal tactics used is character assassination of their opponents. The conduct of a majority of attorneys is such that they should not be allowed to run for political office, and should not be allowed to walk the streets with decent people, or belong to any fraternal and social organization.

Some say maybe this is a sign of the times and due to our declining educational system. However, the problem has been caused by people, and can only be solved by people.

A Midwestern family was devastated in the late 1930s when the father shot and killed a teenager who was teasing him on the main street of the small town. During the trial, the attorney told the wife that he would make sure that the husband would not get the death penalty, for $5,000.00. That was comparable to maybe $100,000.00 today.

The wife sold everything they had to raise the $5,000.00. The attorney changed the charges from murder to manslaughter. The husband was convicted of manslaughter, and of course was paroled after about twenty years. The family after that lived in poverty and depended on state and county welfare the rest of their lives.

Another Midwestern family was devastated when their son was in a car wreck with a friend. The son was severely impaired and took several years to recover. The auto owner's attorneys and insurance company whisked the damaged auto away within a few days, so that it could not be inspected for defects, as one occupant had stated that a wheel came off causing the wreck, but later denied the story. He was evidently influenced by the insurance company attorneys.

A prominent attorney in Alabama related that a case he represented for the plaintiff in Coffee County was going well until the circuit judge changed the jury's makeup after it was approved by both attorneys, and replaced some jurors with some alternate ones who were friendly to the defendant, without ever informing the plaintiff's attorney.

For the first time in history, "outsiders", in other words lawyers and agitators, have flocked to Florida to change the Florida election laws after the election. It is the general opinion that Florida elected officials are capable of running their state and interpreting their own laws.

If you have been observing the courts, there is becoming a greater division between Democrats and Republicans. Judges classify themselves as Liberal (Democrat) or Conservative (Republican), and the same holds about the relationships. Democrat (liberal) judges seem to be more influenced by Democrat attorneys and Republican (conservative) by Republican attorneys.

Judges, although stressing during election/selection that they only interpret the laws, and do not make the laws. But many, in office attempt to make laws and change laws. This is for the legislative branch of government, not the judicial branch.

A friend from Illinois had his complete identification stolen by a trio from Oklahoma. Consequently, several thousand dollars were stolen from his bank account. The trio was caught and tried. They were identified as two prostitutes, and a drug dealer/pimp. The court sentenced the two prostitutes to six months' court supervision, and the other received one year's jail time and one year's court supervision. They were not required to make restitution to the victim. This practice and similar judicial acts are seriously degrading our justice system and is an invitation to criminals that the theft of a person's ID is not a serious crime, drug dealing is not serious, and that pimping and prostitution are okay, because the penalties are insignificant. Is this the message we give to the world and to the next generation?

Chapter IV

MANAGEMENT SUBVERSION

Management subversion has been a little-known activity for thirty years in the military and corporate areas. The following is taken from a paper titled "Research in Organization Theory", October 1970, author unknown. In this group of subversion techniques, the emphasis is placed upon work-oriented methods. This involves the normal day-to-day organizational operations and are most easily implemented by a superior manager.

1. Give him too much work. This involves the piling on of excessive legitimate work, well beyond the capabilities of a normal manager. Care must be taken that the work asked for is managerial and cannot be delegated downwards. If there is even a remote chance of accomplishing all the extra work, double it. This is particularly effective if the work is under outside scrutiny or is due by some well-known deadline date.

2. Take away most of his work. The goal with this technique is to ensure that all the work assigned can be accomplished in a few minutes every day. This technique can be implemented in a multitude of very mechanical ways, such as deleting certain reports due, reassignment of the work to another group, not assigning any new jobs, etc. The goal of this technique is to undermine the individual's sense of purpose within the organization.

3. Nit-pick his correspondence. Refuse to pass on any correspondence until it is letter-perfect. It is particularly aggravating to change sentences and sentence structure so that meaning is warped. If any correspondence does get through unscathed, deliberately red-line a sentence and

write your own comments in red and initial the comments.

4. Delay his correspondence. Do not even read what he writes, nor pay any attention to it. Do nothing, and especially do not pass it on. If information copies have been distributed before you signed the correspondence, call them all back.

5. Borrow his best people. This technique can disrupt the entire group under the manager's control. Assign his best people to "crash jobs" outside of his control. Do not ask permission first, just do it, and tell him about it. This is particularly effective if his best people have established personal relationships with the manager.

6. Low merit raises or salary reviews. According to the pay scale, deliberately give the man a raise low enough to be considered an insult. This can be accompanied with a completely bland performance review.

7. Request fast-response status reports. Every once in a while, ask for a detailed status report on Friday afternoon… due Monday morning. This should be sufficiently detailed to force the man to work over the weekend and disrupt any plans he may have had.

8. Override his decisions. This should be done sporadically, calling your shots. This can be most effective if the decision involves work that the manager had spent a considerable effort completing and one in which he is deeply involved.

9. Company security violation. This can be set up by giving the man's secretary a "company restricted" piece of mail, unmarked as such, late in the afternoon. The first thing the next morning, conduct a department-wide search for the letter and discover it in his in-basket. Do not take any other action, but make sure he knows where the letter was found.

10. Deny or ignore material requisitions. Do not approve any requisitions for supplies, office equipment, or services. Tell him to "make do". If there is justification for the

equipment or material, tell him to "borrow it".

11. Assign work beneath him. This technique demeans the man. Assign him work considerably below his capabilities, and force the man to do it himself. Examples of this method are: manpower histories, checking sick leave requests, etc.

12. Assign the man an assistant. Give him an assistant to "ease his workload". Over a period of time, deliberately task the assistant, talk to him, and generally upgrade the assistant's informal authority. Make sure the manager knows the assistant is "one of your men".

13. Go into excruciating detail. Every time the manager asks for help or gives status reports, get deeply into the detail of what he is doing. Question the reasoning behind each decision. Make it apparent that his performance is under constant scrutiny.

14. Send the man on useless trips. If he dislikes travel, make sure the trips are complex, difficult to conduct, and are frequent enough to keep him off balance. Recruiting trips to college campuses are a good example. Suggest that he does not take his family along. It is even possible to force the man to run up his traveling expenses beyond that which is reasonable for reimbursement. Travel to northern areas in winter can be particularly exasperating.

15. Stop the man's traveling. This is only effective if the manager is used to frequent traveling, and it is part of his normal job. Suggest that he sends somebody else for the really important trips.

16. Question his judgment. In staff meetings especially, cast doubts about his decision-making ability. Make it obvious that, although you will go along with him, you do not agree. If this technique is implemented in the office, make sure his subordinates are within earshot. The objective here is to plant the idea that you do not trust his judgment.

17. Suspend his bonus. If the manager is receiving a managerial-level incentive bonus, temporarily suspend this

benefit for any trivial reason. This is a direct confrontation over basics, so be prepared to justify your reasons.

18. Cut off the informal flow of information. Much of the day-to-day work involves your informal discussions with your subordinates. Deliberately cut the manager off from this source. Make it a point to discuss things in staff meetings which you did not discuss with the manager previously. This will be most effective on topics which are not important, so that the chance of his knowing about them through other sources is slim.

19. Force him to miss staff meetings. If the staff meetings can be scheduled so that you occasionally have them without his presence, the informal transfer of information (see immediately above) can be slowed down.

20. Assign him to a doomed project. Give him work that is destined to failure. This should not be applied to a real go-getter, as he might pull the fat out of the fire and become a department "hero". Assign this onerous work with suggestions that it doesn't really matter if he louses things up, they can't get much worse.

Political Technique

This section covers those factors which can be arbitrarily assigned as political in nature. These involve the continuing jockeying for position that is always going on in any organizational climate. In general, office politics is concerned with the enhancement of a person's status, both informally and formally. There are no rules to obey in office politics, and almost anything goes. An adroit office politician can significantly influence much of the formal work that any department does. If a superior–subordinate relationship does exist, then the superior manager has a distinct advantage... politically... over the subordinate. We can use the authority of his office to back up politically motivated actions.

Office politics is not a game for amateurs. It consists of give-and-take, compromise, and the swift realization of personal opportunity. If the manager, upon which politically oriented strategies are being applied, is an entrenched office politician then the job of removing him by subterfuge will be particularly difficult. In this respect, the victim can use counter-strategies against his superior manager. If the subordinate manager is dull and uncomprehending of political nuances, much of what follows may be a waste of time. The blatancy of the application of politics is dependent upon the particular situation.

1.   Change the performance rating of the manager's subordinates. If he submits a vertically ordered list of the people in his department, based on his evaluation of their performance, deliberately change the ranking just enough to cast doubt on his ability to assess other people.

2.   Don't invite him to all your staff meetings. Deliberately omit an invitation to routine meetings. If you are aware of a request for his presence at outside meetings, go in his place. Do this often enough to jar the continuity of control he may exercise.

3.   Open criticism. This should be done in public, in front of other people, preferably his subordinates. Gentle hints of your discontent are usually enough to set a department buzzing. This technique should be differentiated from a continuous needling on performance. The object here is to reduce the respect his department may have for him.

4.   Violation of line authority. Every once in a while, deliberately go around him on some mundane or technical matter. Go right to his subordinates. Do not bother to inform him, of the fact, even after the fact. Any technical information picked up in this manner can be used later as a club in your hands, especially if he is trying to cover something up.

5.   Borrow his secretary. This is especially effective if his secretary has been with him for a long time. The ultimate blow would be to replace her with an incompetent girl. Borrowing his secretary for periods of time long enough to disrupt his normal office routine is best. If this can be time-phased during known periods of heavy secretarial workloads, all to the best.

6. Promote one of his subordinates without his prior knowledge. This will have the effect of frustrating any ranking procedures he may have in effect. If you can take advantage of any personal conflicts within his department, this ploy will be traumatic.

7. Force him to take vacation prematurely. This can be prefaced with a forecasted crash job, or some other pretext. A corollary to this would be to force a last-minute cancellation of vacation plans.

8. Get him involved in an unsolvable personal problem. From department history, it should be easy to determine where personnel conflicts exist. Sending the manager in to settle long-standing disputes should rekindle old hatreds. This type of intervention can only be interpreted as meddling, so the manager cannot solve anything. A particularly good opportunity might develop if the manager takes sides.

9. Force him to take a stand on a union issue and then back away. This can be most effective if the issue is not clear. Let him interpret company policy and enact it, and then offer grudging support, complaining that you have been forced to compromise company policy because of a subordinate's actions. If the issue gets to the grievance state, a forum is already prepared to demean your subordinate.

10. Load his department with troublemakers. If you have the authority to maneuver the people under you, a gradual shifting of the known troublemakers into the manager's department will make life miserable for him. Troublemakers such as union radicals, religious zealots, psychological problems, etc., cannot be effectively controlled by a normal manager. This ploy will lay the groundwork for future internal problems within his group.

11. Use his prejudices against him. If the manager has a few particular personal prejudices, these can be effectively used to precipitate obvious blunders on his part. As an example, assign him the task of performing a detailed study

into some technical or managerial area about which you know he has preconceived ideas. Unless he is unusually objective, his personal feelings will become part of the study effort. These feelings can be used as clubs against him to discredit the study effort.

12. Cut back his group until he is over-managing. This can be done by directing a personnel layoff in his group, without his concurrence, to the point where his group rebels at the increased workload and increased meddling into individual job situations on his part. Requests for transfers should also increase under conditions such as this. The result will be frustration.

13. Bring in a watchdog group to look over his shoulder. In most companies, there is some form of management auditing or value analysis group which is charged with the responsibility of evaluating departmental performance. The presence of outside interference such as this is unnerving. The very point that you brought the outside group in is indicative to others that you are dissatisfied with performance. The danger in this approach lies in the fact that spin-off from any audit might detract from your managerial department, and unless the audit pinpoints specific managerial problems in his group, this could be damaging to you.

14. Withhold managerial privileges. This technique affronts the status symbology system in force. Good examples are the withholding of prime parking spaces, withholding new office appurtenances, not having his office painted, etc.

15. Confide specific information to his secretary and not to him. This is particularly effective if the information is policy related or has to do with personnel work. What is desired here is that he will "get the word" from his secretary and not directly from you. This will enhance his secretary's prestige at the cost of his. This will also trigger the grapevine and announce via the informal organization structure that you are dissatisfied with his performance.

16. Make an obvious display of your interest in his work.

Keep his internal records on your desk. Make it obvious to him that he is being evaluated continually. This might be used at times of the year when there is no apparent reason for this interest... just after a pay raise was issued, for instance.

17. Repetitive development interviews. This is similar to 16 above, but is different in the fact that you are constantly harping on his managerial deficiencies. This is a heavy-handed way of alerting him to your displeasure. Intangibles are particularly amenable to this technique... such as human relations, union relations, initiative, etc.

18. Accuse him of being unethical. If there is any cause for doubt about a particular decision he has made, accuse him of unethical conduct. This strikes directly at his moral fiber. Of course, if the entire organization is basically unethical, this technique is of no value.

19. Frequent office moves. Move his department or his office around enough to disrupt his normal functioning. The chaos resulting from frequent moves can result in substandard performance. This technique can be augmented with frequent telephone number changes, which effectively cut him off from routine communication channels. If the size of the office is a status symbol, this can be juggled accordingly.

20. Set up an ethnic problem for which a known prejudice exists. This technique employs his own weaknesses to discredit him. Examples are numerous. If he is a hard-core southerner, for instance, force him to work with (or for) colored people. Religious prejudices can also be used in the same way. These types of situations are ugly, and the unfortunate part is that any dire consequences might rub off on you.

Chapter V
USE OF PROFESSIONAL ENGINEERS

We can all give credit to the engineering community for virtually everything we touch. Engineers have accomplished more than any other profession in existence today. The Professional Engineers in Private Practice (PEPP), Professional Engineers in Construction (PEC), Professional Engineers in Industry (PEI) have been the leaders in this technical revolution. Professional Engineers in Government (PEG) are probably the most distraught of all engineers. Most engineers who are supervised by non-engineers are not utilized to their full capacity.

In April 1986, the national chairman of Professional Engineers in Government (PEG) released the following article.

FEDERAL ENGINEERS; AN ENDANGERED SPECIES

As this country moves toward an increasingly technology-driven economy, much of the basic research and development burden alls squarely on the broad shoulders of the federal government. Given this responsibility to the national interests, shouldn't the federal government employ the strongest cadre of engineers and scientists available?

Yes, it should—but so, it doesn't.

The reason is fundamental: the current compensation and personnel practices of the federal government do not make public sector employment at the federal level an attractive career option. In fact, the current system provides a disincentive to qualified engineers and scientists to enter the federal workforce.

Without an adequate supply of qualified engineering talent, our nation's public works infrastructure, space program, federal laboratories and other critical areas will not be able to meet this nation's technological needs.

Generally speaking, there are four areas in the government into which the majority of engineering positions fall: research and development, acquisition and project management, design and regulation.

As vital as these areas are to our government's efficient management and to the nation's future, in too many situations, these engineering positions have been filled by either less than fully qualified engineers or non-engineers.

While there are many outstanding engineers throughout the government, all too frequently individuals who fill key engineering positions lack the experience or educational background to handle complex engineering jobs. Because of an inability to attract top engineering applicants, agencies, laboratories and other federal institutions are often forced to hire engineers of second choice—those who are not in demand by industry or the private sector.

Once on board, the career ladder system of the civil service takes over, promoting them to positions which sometimes exceed their abilities and training.

At the National Society of Professional Engineers, we hear of many examples of this flawed process. Here is one example.

An engineering technology graduate with approximately half of the required course work to be considered eligible for an engineering position was given a GS-5 rating upon entering the government. Within thirty months he was promoted to a GS-11 engineering position.

The individual's supervisor became aware that the employee could not perform even the most basic engineering "tasks", yet rather than being demoted to a less responsible position, he was simply transferred to another engineering group. This inability to satisfactorily deal with the problem is typical and inherently self-destructive.

In the acquisition area, private sector engineers under contract to the federal government often find themselves dealing with people who don't have the technical background to understand the complicated million-dollar contracts for which they are contracting. This results in not only administrative problems for both the contractors and the government, but also a potentially unsatisfactory and inadequate product. Government contracting officers must be supported by objective, technical expertise.

Unfortunately, compared with other professional opportunities available to young engineers, the government just does not compete, given the personnel and compensation system now in place. This problem is not just limited to entry-level positions. It is equally difficult to lure prominent, senior-level engineers and scientists into top jobs in the government. Perhaps most difficult is the ability to retain top quality mid-level engineers.

These observations are borne out in a 1984 Government Accounting Office report which found that federally employed engineers experienced a pay disparity of 47 percent below the private sector at the entry level, and 25 percent below at the GS-11 level.

The current system of special pay rates for certain federal employees (about 19,000, or 52 percent of the total, are engineers and scientists) has failed to address the problem. This system, originally intended as a stop-gap measure to allow the government to compete with the private sector, has been a dismal failure. Now in existence for more than ten years, it has been a Band-Aid approach to a problem needing radical surgery.

Under the special pay rates system, the task of evaluating agency and departmental needs often does not involve input from the technical managers. Further complicating the process is the repeated generic use of the term "engineer" to describe government positions ranging from technicians and technologists to graduate-level engineers and licensed professional engineers.

Even OPM's basic qualifications standards work against staffing engineering positions adequately. Under a system of "alternate methods," an engineering technician can become an engineer in the federal government without an engineering degree, provided he or she accomplishes a certain amount of college-level education in a related field, and has at least one year of professional engineering experience acquired under professional engineering supervision and guidance.

A parallel example would be an individual completing four years of training as a nurse and then, after working for a year as a surgical assistant, being cleared by the government to perform open heart surgery.

Once an individual becomes an engineer under this alternate method, he or she is listed as experienced as an engineer, despite a lack of hard skills and an inadequate education. They are further in a position to move into managerial positions, in many cases with oversight of trained and licenses professional engineers.

Clearly, the special pay rate system has done little to improve the compensation of federal engineers and scientists, as it was mentioned earlier, and would seem to have had a deleterious effect on the quality of government engineering services.

In July 1985, President Reagan appointed a Blue Ribbon Commission on Defense Management and charged it to study

America's current defense management and organization. Informally dubbed the Packard Commission, after chairman David Packard, the interim report was presented to the president on February 18, 1986. The commission was quite succinct in its analysis for improving acquisition organization:

"To attract and retain a good workforce requires a more flexible system for management of contracting officers and other senior acquisition personnel—one comparable to the successful system for scientists and engineers recently demonstrated at the Navy's China Lake Laboratory... The Commission's recommendations in this critical area can and should be acted upon quickly and are of the highest priority... More money and better engineering invested at the front end will get more reliable and better performing weapons into the field more quickly and cheaply."

The commission further recommended that "an alternate personnel management system, modeled on the China Lake Laboratory demonstration project, could be established to include senior acquisition personnel and contracting officers as well as scientists and engineers."

Now that President Reagan has endorsed the recommendations, it would seem the time to make some substantive changes to this difficult and cumbersome system is now.

There has been legislation offered by Rep. Don Fuqua (D-Fla.) and Sen. Jeff Bingaman (D.N.M.), (H.R. 3480 and S.1727 respectively), which addresses the problem not only as it affects engineers and scientists in the Department of Defense, but across government. It directs each agency to develop and implement its own program, changing to meet the diverse needs and resources of its particular institution. It would also create broad pay bands allowing managers then flexibility to reward top performers and encourage improvement across the board.

Two additional recommendations will strengthen these and/or other pieces of legislation aimed at improving the federal government's engineering services:

First, there should be specific definitions of engineering and scientific personnel, with rigorous, well-defined educational requirements, and preferable, licensure as a professional engineer.

Second, place the responsibility of evaluating technical personnel not with the agency executives and personnel lists, but with the technical managers who can better evaluate the performance of the technical employee.

As Congress and the executive branch continue to deliberate the merits of reforming the federal personnel and compensation systems, the National Society of Professional Engineers hopes the above thoughts will not go totally unnoticed.

The failure to address this dilemma will serve to prolong the "brain drain" our government suffers, as more and more of our leading engineers and scientists leave, and our brightest young minds will continue to think of government service as a career choice of last resort.

Previously, in November 1983, a paper was released entitled "Why Can't We Recruit Good Engineers in the Federal Government".

We have all read some of the attacks launched against federal employees. Professional engineers fall within the same pay scale as other federal employees. Professional engineers have not only completed some of the toughest college programs, but have passed one of the most difficult tests of any profession. So why do we have difficulty in recruiting engineers, especially new graduates?

First, we can't offer the salaries that private industry can. One recruiter from an army personnel office recently stated that "he felt like crawling under the table" when he was between two other recruiters at a major university. On one side, the recruiter was offering over $24,000 per year and the other was offering just under $24,000, as beginning salaries. The army recruiter could offer only $17,000 per year except for honor graduates and Master degree graduates. Under the special pay scale for engineers these honor and Master degree graduates could be offered up to about $21,527. However, these special graduates cold easily go into industry at $26,000–$28,000 per year.

Secondly, benefits for federal employees have been eroded, while benefits in industry have been increasing. Most of the government pay raises have not kept pace either with the cost of living, inflation rate, or industry. Also, grade level caps established in the government and demand in industry have discouraged several engineers from staying in government service.

A recent survey of federal executives reflected that 71 percent would advise competent young people to seek careers in the private sector; 58 percent were generally pessimistic about prospects for rewarding government careers in the next ten to fifteen years; and one-third said they did not expect to be with their present organization three years from now.

The present thirty year-age fifty-five and disability retirement programs, with options, are the main "selling points" for federal service. Next are the annual leave and sick leave programs. When social security takes effect on January 1, 1984, even with a supplemental Civil Service plan, it may be even more difficult to recruit and retain quality engineers.

Already, the shortage of engineers is causing non-engineers to perform engineering tasks, thereby lowering the quality of end-products. Among these non-engineers are technicians, mathematicians, psychologists, and a host of other non-engineers. This poses a problem for engineers subordinate to non-engineers who do not and never will understand what engineering is all about.

Another syndrome that exists in many government activities is that engineers are not managers. This also exists in industry. The truth is that junior engineers should be encouraged and supported in obtaining the experience and training appropriate for advancing to management positions.

Restrictions are getting tighter on attendance at seminars and symposiums. An Alabama Survey of PEG, reflected that 58 percent attended no seminars/symposiums. Fifty-seven percent of these were DOD engineers. Some were attended by one-third of those polled, and 14.2 percent attended several.

Professional treatment of engineers working for engineers was excellent to good for 50 percent, while those working for non-engineers rated 25 percent excellent to good and 25 percent fair. Those working for engineers rated their treatment only in the excellent and good categories. Whether supervisors were military or civilian had no bearing.

So, what can we do to get out of this dilemma in government? Merit pay and basing pay on performance of government engineers are definitely not the answer in the federal government. Non-engineers are prejudiced. Engineers are not given the proper level of authority they are capable of. Jealousy against professional engineers is widespread among non-engineer supervisors.

If the federal government is interested in hiring and retaining good engineers, the following are highly recommended, from a management viewpoint, for success of federal government projects and programs.

1. Engineers and scientists must be separated from the general schedule. Beginning salaries should be based on the going rate of industry. 1983 statistics show that the entry

level of GS-5 should be in the neighborhood of $24,000 per year. Industry statistics should be used upward from the entry level, to approximately $75,000 per year for a career GS-15 engineer who entered government service between GS-5 and GS-12. (The reason for the $75,000 figure is that there are two GS-15 R&D engineers who left government service, one for $95,000 and another at $75,000 per year.)

2. They should be required to attend at least two professional seminars/technical meetings per year at government expense.

3. They should be reimbursed up to $300 per year for professional membership dues and allowed TDY expenses for attending one annual convention for each professional organization they are leaders or officers in, or are technology oriented.

4. N.S.P.E. should have a "hotline" for reporting fraud, disrespect or maltreatment of engineers. Reports could be turned over to the appropriate agency for investigation.

Also, in 1984, a survey was made of Professional Engineers in Government in Alabama:

The fall 1983 survey of Professional Engineers in Government (PEG), Alabama Society of Professional Engineers (ASPE), reflected some of the reasons the federal government is having trouble in recruiting and retaining high quality engineers.

Attendance (at employers expense) at professional symposiums and seminars was one of the most interesting categories. Of the total reported, 46.6 percent attended none, 46.6 percent attended some, and 6.6 percent attended several. County and city accounted for 14.3 percent. The DOD represented 83.3 percent of federal engineers. In the "some" category, 71.4 percent were federal and 28.6 percent were state, county and city. Military organizations accounted for 20 percent of the federal, and 80 percent were state, county, and city. "Some" were considered two to four per year. Several (four or more per year) were attended by 6.7 percent and all of these were city engineers.

Professional treatment: the study was divided into three levels; DOD represented 53.3 percent, other federal 26.4 percent and local 20 percent. Rankings were classified as excellent, good, fair and poor. Rating of job satisfaction was further divided into military and civilian supervision. Military supervision represented 37.5 percent of DOD engineers. One-third of those supervised by military rated their treatment excellent (all supervisors were engineers) and 66 percent rated treatment as fair (all supervised by non-engineers.)

Engineers supervised by civilians constituted 62.5 percent of the DOD group. Twenty percent rated treatment excellent and 60 percent rated it good. One half of excellent ratings were supervised by engineers and all that rated treatment "good" were supervised by engineers. One half of respondents working for DOD would recommend their employer to a graduating engineer.

Other federal engineers rated their treatment excellent (75 percent) and fair (25 percent). Those rating treatment as excellent were all supervised by engineers and the 25 percent who rated treatment fair were supervised by non-engineers. Three-fourths would recommend their employer to a graduating engineer. The 25 percent who would not recommend their employer were almost all supervised by non-engineers.

Engineers employed by state, county or city rated their treatment one-third excellent, one-third good and one-third fair. Two-thirds were supervised by non-engineers, and two-thirds would recommend their employer to a graduating engineer, but there was no direct correlation.

Responses were almost evenly divided between veterans and non-veterans. State and city engineers were predominately non-veterans, and county engineers were predominately veterans. However, over 58 percent of federal engineers are veterans and 62.5 percent of DOD engineers are veterans.

Training opportunities were rated good by 33.3 percent, fair by 53.3 percent and poor by 13.3 percent. There was no correlation to any level of government.

Authority was rated as adequate by 53.3 percent, ranging in salary from $10,000 to $50,000. Full authority ranged from $30,000 to $50,000 although it constituted only 20 percent of respondents. Inadequate technical authority was granted to 13.3 percent, ranging in salary $30,000 to over $50,000. These were all within DOD, and were correlated to non-engineer military supervisors.

Years later, in November 2000, we face some of the same

problems as the early 1980s, but no level of government is willing to change. The following is taken from a national publication, November 2000.

Professional engineers in government would like to think that they have the final say when it comes to engineering decisions made in the interest of public health, safety, and welfare. After all, many believe that protecting the public from design failures was the reason for licensure laws in the first place.

Nevertheless, it's not unusual for a non-engineer to hold a high position in government overseeing an engineering-related department. More troubling to engineers across the country are the reported cases of non-engineers replacing P.E.s in government positions and, in the worst cases, influencing or making engineering decisions that they may not be qualified to deliver. Some engineers have taken a stand, although it seems that more have not. And although rules may outline the qualifications for certain high-ranking engineering positions in government, P.E.s say that in many cases, politically connected individuals get the last word.

The other side of the argument is that individuals who may not be P.E.s—but possess exceptional leadership, communication, and business skills—can lead a department of engineers more effectively than P.E.s if they are not performing engineering and are stronger in these other key areas.

Engineering groups have challenged the appointment of non-engineers to positions formerly held by P.E.s in several notable situations. Two years ago, the Detroit City Council questioned the mayoral appointment of Geni Giannotti, a certified public accountant, to lead the city's Building and Safety Engineering Department. Some council members said that the appointment violated the city ordinance because Giannotti had no engineering background or experience. The mayor's office, however, argues that amendments to the ordinance allowed Giannotti to continue in the position.

When the Michigan Society of Professional Engineers raised the issue with the mayor's office, it was assured that Giannotti's responsibility was to manage people, not perform engineering. But many P.E.s remained unconvinced that anyone except a licensed engineer should be in charge of an engineering department. Giannotti is still in office today, backed by the city's claims that she is only a manager and has assigned engineering responsibilities to her subordinates.

Last year in Kansas, P.E.s' protests went unheard as the state enacted a bill that took away some of the decision-making authority of the chief engineer of the Water Resources Division of the State Department of Agriculture. The law transferred rule-making authority to the state's agriculture secretary land required the chief engineer to answer to the secretary, a non-engineer. Before this law passed, the chief engineer's decisions were final and could be appealed only through district court.

In some cases, engineers have been able to change the decision to fill a P.E. position with a non-engineer, however. Members of the Hawaii Society of Professional Engineers submitted oral and written testimony against a proposed county charter amendment that would have eliminated the P.E. requirement for the head of the Public Works Department, who holds the title of chief engineer, and the manager of the Department of Water Supply. Recently, H.S.P.E. received word from the Hawaii County Charter Commission that the proposed amendment was killed before it could get out of the commission and onto the ballot.

"We also understand that the rejection of the amendment was in large part due to the testimony in opposition by Big Island licensed professional engineers," says H.S.P.E. president and P.E. Curtis Beck, one of the engineers who testified. Subsequently, professional engineer Robert Yanabu was hired for the position of chief engineer of Hawaii County.

One the East Coast, the New York State Society of Professional Engineers' Queens Chapter has joined with other members of the A/E community to propose to mayoral candidates a reorganization of city positions that gives licensed A/Es a greater role in infrastructure management. Professional engineer Salvatore Galleta, president of the Queens Chapter, hoped to get the proposal out to the candidates for their review by the end of October.

The proposal recommends that the city charter be revised to add two key positions, a deputy mayor for infrastructure and an engineer general, which would be filled by P.E.s or registered architects. It also calls for commissioners of city agencies that perform A/E work, such as the Department of Transportation and the Department of Environmental Protection, to be P.E.s or registered architects. After the candidates have a chance to endorse it, A/Es plan to unveil the proposal in a press conference preceding the November 2001 elections. "We are counting on mayoral candidates to take this proposal and make it one of the major issues of the campaign," says Galleta.

He adds that he is familiar with many situations in government in which P.E.s are replaced or supervised by non-engineers in engineering departments. "It used to be that just the top positions were politically appointed, but now it's going further into lower ranks," Galleta says. "The public in general and politicians in particular do not seem to appreciate the importance of engineering... If there haven't been collapses and disasters, the profession is taken almost as a matter of course."

N.S.P.E.'s Professional Engineers in Government conducted a survey of P.E.s in government positions to find out about cases in which engineers were replaced with non-engineers or engineering positions were downgraded and supervision became a non-engineer responsibility. PEG found that it is not uncommon, according to survey respondents, for positions formerly held by P.E.s such as "public works director," to be filled by non-engineers.

As the former executive director of the Texas licensing board, professional engineer John Speed says, "I can tell you far more horror stories than you would like to hear about situations where non-engineers were 'directors of public works' or 'engineering supervisors' in communities."

One "horror story" told by another P.E. involved a non-engineer public works director who retained a retired bridge inspector to look at a bridge that had serious structural problems. According to the P.E., insufficient adjustments were made to the bridge and traffic was allowed to pass over it. He believed that the bridge was in danger of falling.

Another engineer reported "overt and persistent retaliation" for refusing to sign and approve unwarranted waivers to regulations affecting public safety and the environment. Other survey participants reported the downgrading of top departmental positions that could only be held by P.E.s to positions filled by non-engineers—sometimes, they believed, in violation of laws or ordinances.

Some of those engineers who provided examples for the survey did not wish to be identified. When engineers are willing to climb into the hot seat on this issue, one difficulty is then finding concrete evidence that the lack of qualifications of a non-engineer in charge was the prime cause of a public works failure.

"While it is possible (and maybe likely) that decisions of professional engineers have been overturned by their non-engineer superiors, we are not necessarily notified when those conditions occur," says professional land surveyor George Twiss, executive director of the Washington state licensing board. "It would also be very difficult to attribute such occurrences as the sole cause of a project failure. Our experience would suggest that multiple issues are usually involved."

One of those factors is an individual's ability to lead a department and motivate a diverse group of professionals. Although he believes that the current directors of engineering departments in his area are P.E.s, Myron Calkins, a professional engineer and former Kansas City director of public works, says the "writing is on the wall" because "not a lot of engineers today have a good grasp of management requirements". He adds that top spots will be open to non-engineers if qualified P.E.s do not acquire more of the right communications and business skills.

The reflection on how engineers are utilized is evidenced by the quality and mismanagement in many products and services we receive. In a society where the unemployment rate is very low, capable managers are next to impossible to hire, and consequently non-engineers are not using engineering talent and capability in the decision and management process. This is also true of highly experienced technicians who have their recommendations overridden by administrators.

For example, an experienced tool and die maker was told by the company manager, whose experience was managing hospices, to machine the tool to specifications before heat treating. The technician told him that it had to be heat treated before final machining, because the heat treatment would alter the specifications. The plant manager directed the technician to final machine the tool and then heat treat. The technician complied, and the tool was below specifications. The tool had to be refabricated, as a result of this, the tool and die maker was laid off, replaced with a lower paid trainee, and the plant closed approximately one year after. Although this individual is not an engineer, it reflects how even highly qualified technicians are not utilized properly.

A federal engineer, one of the highest qualified in the federal government, was professionally and personally attacked on, to rout him out of his position. Other engineers working in the organization were not recognized and would not stay. The emphasis was put on psychologists, who claimed engineering experience, were classified as Engineering Psychologists and Operations Research Analysts (ORSA), for which engineers are more qualified for ORSA than psychologists and other disciplines due to the high mathematical ability and training.

After the top engineer of the organization was forced into disability retirement, the unit was abolished. This was an example of management subversion (see Chapter IV).

Most federal and industry engineers are hoping to hang on until retirement, although several may not be able to.

The most dissatisfaction is among government engineers who are supervised by non-engineers, either military or civilian.

Chapter VI

BANKING AND FINANCE, INSURANCE, ENERGY AND ENVIRONMENT

Banking and Finance

Some of us remember when the local bank was friendly and all the officers knew the customers by name. If you needed a loan, they were at your service, and the bank president could make a decision on the spot, because he already knew what your assets were, your ethical standards, and your repayment capability. It was made mostly based on assets owned.

Presently, most banks have consolidated and/or been purchased by large banking corporations. The services have decreased to the point where you are charged for almost all services. The next charge that is probably on the horizon is a charge for speaking to a teller, or other officer. This will not be a small charge, but most likely based on salary, overhead, and profit. These mega-corporations have access to all credit reports, and flood our mail with credit card offers and blank checks.

For example, they offer 0 percent for a few months "to get you hooked" and a fixed rate for transfers and purchases. After about three months at a fixed rate of 9.9 percent, you get a notice that the interest rate is changed to 17.98 percent, due to a review of your credit report. You get your free copy of your credit report, it is the same as for the past four years, not even any late payment, change in income/payment ratio, but income has increased during this period.

You then attempt to call the customer service number, and get electronic answering. None of the options fit the question you have. You frequently get a busy signal, or the number just doesn't answer. If you are lucky enough to get a person's mailbox, that person is never available, or the mailbox is full.

You cancel the credit card account and every week or two you get letters relative to your account, and periodically a sheet of checks to write on your account. It takes sometimes two or three letters to the bank to get the account closed and cease the sending of unsolicited checks.

One year you purchase a home and the local bank president is eager and does anything he can to expedite the loan. Three years later, after the bank has been sold to a large bank, with headquarters 500 miles away, it is a different story.

The local president and board have no authority except administrative and personnel management. All loan papers (twenty-five or thirty) have to be sent by fax from the distant bank. All approvals are taken over by the distant bank, and the quality of the loan package is severely degraded.

All approvals are taken over by the distant bank, and the quality of the loan package is severely degraded.

Your retirement check automatic deposits now go to the district bank, and all checks written on your account are cleared through the distant headquarters and not through the local bank. The service of the local bank is seriously degraded.

In bank mergers, the principal bank curtails services to save costs. They consolidate processing approvals and loan servicing at the distant bank, which is what causes degradation of services and fewer local jobs.

When your loan closes, one of the documents you sign relates to selling the mortgage to a New York bank, before the loan is closed. Thus you thought you were supporting the local economy, but you are the victim of the new banking activities.

Remember when we had a coupon book to pay our payment monthly? Not now. Many large banks are sending monthly statements. For example, maybe it costs $8.00 to print a payment coupon book. With postage now at thirty-seven cents, or maybe less for bulk mailing, this still doesn't make good sense for a thirty-year mortgage. Although the average mortgage is refinanced or changed every ten years, the cost for postage is still three times the cost of a coupon book. Maybe they don't intend to hold the mortgage that long, with the selling, swapping, etc. in the banking industry.

Another example is a family who contracted to sell their house and purchase another. They found a buyer and the home financing company in Jacksonville, FL, with the understanding that the buyer could assume the mortgage.

The family purchased another house under the understanding the assumption could be completed within ninety days or less. The ninety days passed, they obtained an extension to the contract for the new house. Many telephone calls ensued and no one in the mortgage company would tell any details. They just told them that it was in process and should be completed in thirty days.

Incidentally, they could seldom reach a loan officer. When they called the loan company, the electronic answering would transfer to the mailbox for the section handling loan assumptions. Then, either they received the message that the mailbox was full, or if they were fortunate to get into the mailbox, they were told that someone would return their call in twenty-four to forty-eight hours. The return call seldom occurred.

This ensued for a total of 150 days, the purchaser of their home backed out, and the family had to borrow family money to purchase the new home until they could sell their previous home.

Also related to the banking industry and to Internet purchases, is identity theft. There have been many cases of significant losses by users of bank cards, ATM cards, driver's licenses, charge cards and debit cards. Thus, everyone should be overly conscious of card and driver's license numbers ending up in the wrong hands. One case in point is when using a credit card for Internet purchase, make sure you are on a secure connection. Several are getting their social security number deleted from their driver's license. Also, there is widespread theft of blank checks. If you should become a victim of this scam, immediately change all your account numbers at your bank and notify law enforcement.

The credit card company will provide little help in case of credit card number theft. By all means, do not provide your social security or bank account numbers to anyone calling on the telephone.

If you are in business, you may think that wholesale and retail credit companies are on your side. Think again, they are in favor of the manufacturer. If you have a problem with the manufacturer or distributor, the credit companies will take the side of the manufacturer or distributor.

Many people seem to be heading for a major disaster. The average college student had a balance of over $1,800.00 a year ago and over $2,700.00 in the first part of 2001 on charge cards. In 2001, the average credit card balance was $8,500.00, the highest in history. There is a large amount of families taking a second mortgage to refinance other debts. There is a day of reckoning when they reach the limit and have no place to go. Thus they face the prospect of losing their home when the other debts pile up again. Remember, the banking and finance companies have no mercy. Remember free checking? It is becoming a thing of the past as more banks charge for each deposit, each check, and most other services. We will probably be charged for drive-in service and counter service in the near future.

Your best bet is credit unions, most offer better service and competitive rates.

Insurance

For many years the insurance companies have been labeled as owning this country. In other words, the large insurance companies have made millions, and several small companies have been purchased by the larger companies. However, it is impossible to find which companies were purchased by large companies. For example one company was termed as nonexistent when a claim was ready to be submitted. No one could tell if they just went bankrupt or were bought by a large company. Some that had gone bankrupt were purchased by large companies, but the larger company was not liable for claims against the other company. A common term is "restructuring", which throws the policyholder into a turmoil. For example, you pay into a life insurance policy for fifteen years. The policyholder dies, and the family cannot locate the company due to this restructuring—merging or reorganization and name change. Remember, everything is based on money and companies will endeavor to make the most out of policyholders.

There are several reputable companies in existence. One of the best is your farm bureau, or similar state coop. In any case, you must choose the most reasonable source of insurance, but not forget the most reputable.

Another aspect is casualty insurance including business and vehicle. Some insurance companies have their own adjusters and will probably be your best bet for vehicle insurance. Others hire adjustment companies to settle their claims, and this is where you get cheated.

For example, a dealer had property insurance which was referred to as a reputable company by the manufacturer. They were good on small claims but when a major disaster struck, it took over three months through an adjustment company and the dealer got shortchanged by approximately $30,000.00, which caused him to go out of business. If they had been fair with him, he could have reopened and continued business. The parent company is one of the most respected companies in farm and lawn equipment. Another subordinate company is a highly reputable finance company, but the insurance subordinate is a discredit to the other company subordinates.

An accident insured by the individual at fault is another example of clandestine operations. The day of the accident, the victim attempted to locate the insurance company. They were not listed in the Atlanta, GA, directory, and required the company to go state wide for information. After many phone calls, a listing was found in Athens, GA. The adjustment representation was finally located, after the police report was obtained, and the insured's auto had been removed from the towing company lot. The area code for Atlanta is 404 and the area code finally located was 770, and the fax number is area code 912.

The costs associated on the part of the victim were presented ($5,542.48). The two trucks damaged were approved and the insurance paid $4,260.00 (more or less in dollars) for repair. The other costs on trailer damage, extra labor, mileage, extra meals, lodging would not be approved for payment as of one month later. The checks were issued by another insurance company.

The adjustors do not seem interested in satisfying their customers, and it seems that the bottom line is that they are uneducated, inexperienced, and incapable of being fair and objective.

Health insurance and costs have skyrocketed. The HMOs were organized with their main goal as profit. They have been paying officials exorbitant salaries and do their best to cheat the policyholder.

Medical costs have skyrocketed due to exorbitant salaries of officers in the large hospital/medical organizations. The conglomerates that have bought up the hospitals are contracted to manage hospital operations, spend money like there is no limit, while reducing costs by sacrificing health care, putting more workload on nurses and aides, reducing care staffs to the point that we are facing a shortage of nurses.

Energy

We have all heard of controversial groups demonstrating on a variety of issues. The California rolling blackouts are an example of the result. Also, the Environmental Protection Agency has greatly hampered the progress, not only with electricity but other areas as well.

California Electric companies have not built any new power generator facilities in the past ten years and none are under construction. Thus, citizens of California have not seen the worst yet. It takes about ten to fifteen years to get a new power plant on line. The anti-nuclear groups are partly responsible for this. The nuclear power plants are the safest and most economical. The entire western United States has been depending on lakes for power generation for years. Now the lakes are drying up from lack of rainfall and increased water demands.

As one former Californian resident remarked, "California's mess is their own making. The legislature deregulated utilities without thinking things out. The law required direct suppliers to customers to get rid of their power plants and not to build any more. But the population continued to skyrocket, houses bloomed up everywhere and the demand for energy increased exponentially while utilities had to, and continue to have to, buy power from the antiquated plants they sold and from distant plants."

The suppliers of utilities have been gouging their customers. This also added another layer of bureaucrats and profits. It has been reported that the suppliers have been selling a lot of their power production out of the state. This with all the wealth and technology in California, the legislature does not use logical thinking.

The rush to deregulation, as appealing as it sounds to the populace and information from the "spin doctors", has been and still is foolhardy. This will probably extend to water for irrigation, and be devastating to the Californian economy.

Adam Smith, the father of capitalism, wrote in his *Wealth of Nations* that you have to be suspicious of any combination, at lunch or otherwise, of businessmen in the same business because they, as all of us, are victors of their own venality and are apt to fix prices, raise prices in unison, stifle competition, etc. The power situation is an egregious example.

The main drawback is that California's retail power costs are frozen, while the wholesale prices are deregulated. This threatens the retail power providers with bankruptcy, if they are not "bailed out" by some entity.

The oil and gas system is a disaster for the United States and a boom for OPEC. OPEC flooded the U.S. market with oil when imports by the U.S. was about 38 percent. The crude oil prices were driven to about seven to nine dollars per barrel. The U.S. cost of production was sixteen to eighteen dollars a barrel. Consequently many independent operators, who produced almost 80 percent of U.S. production, were driven into bankruptcy and many low-producing wells were abandoned.

Drilling companies and oil well service companies were driven out of business. About one-half of the drilling rigs were cut up and recycled. Many experienced personnel were forced to seek other careers.

When OPEC saw the right time, they lowered their production quotas and drove the crude oil price to thirty-to thirty-four dollars per barrel. Thus the percentage of imports jumped to 70 percent.

The Energy Department of the U.S. government is partly to blame as well as some states like Illinois who have overdone the environmental issues and forced many lower-producing wells to be closed.

In one case the operator could not afford to maintain the wells at seven or eight dollars per barrel. The State Oil and Gas Division inspectors closed the wells for some minor environmental concerns. When the oil price increased and the operator tried to reopen the wells, the state had charges and liens on the wells, so they could not be reopened. Then the state instigated a program whereby the landowners could obtain state grants to have the wells "plugged".

Over the past several years the exploration has almost ceased due to the policies of the Illinois Oil and Gas Division and the uncertainty of oil prices. The independent operators produced 70 to 80 percent of the oil in the U.S.

As a result oil well service companies such as Halliburton, Dowell and Schlumberger have almost ceased operation in the south central area of Illinois and could "blight" areas in once busy areas. All this can be traced back to the U.S. Energy Department, the state and large oil companies, which have almost ruined the oil business in these areas, which can be termed as political maneuvering.

No new refineries have been built in the past ten years and old refineries have been closed. The main problem presently is the operating refineries are operating at near capacity.

As far as the Illinois Oil and Gas Division is concerned, it is a complete disaster. Wells that can now be producing are classified as abandoned, and the landowner gets funds from the state to "plug" the wells, without any concern nor notification to the operators and royalty owners. When contacted, they would not send documentation, listen to the operators and royalty owners, and would not even have the courtesy to return calls. The individuals are very seldom available and use their voice mail as an excuse. There are also indications that the local inspector, oil well service company and the landowner may be guilty of fraud.

Part of the blame can be attributed to the philosophy of the administration in the 1990s, which were against fossil fuels, in favor of developing solar systems and windmills. They thought that if the price of fossil fuels was high, it would cause development of other sources.

We have a surplus of coal which could be used if we only would develop cleaner burning of coal for power.

The lack of exploration for natural gas will probably haunt us in the future. New power plants are gas-powered and the increase in usage due to electricity problems will significantly increase. Gas exploration is the same as oil—almost non existent—so watch out for higher prices and shortages.

Heating oil, diesel fuel and all other derivatives of crude oil are in the same situation.

The incentive for new exploration is the depletion allowance. Since it was decreased from 40 percent to 15 percent, independent oil production has almost ceased due to the lack of investment incentives.

Some of the answers are:

1. Increase the depletion allowance to 35–40 percent for small producers.

2. States must not be allowed to plug and "steal" the equipment for older wells that can be produced.

3. Oil companies must channel the funds to build more refineries as soon as possible.

4. There are rumors that most of the Alaskan oil is being sold to Russia. This should be investigated.

Environment

Our environment has been tainted by industry which for several years have "dumped" hazardous waste into sewers, streams, rivers and the oceans. Every day we hear of high levels of some chemical discovered in residential areas, and fish from streams, rivers and the ocean being tainted.

We have had government officials at all levels hired to enforce standards and to ensure that our food and water are safe. However, the use of bottled water has ballooned over the past few years and is expected to grow.

Many young people are now having kidney problems, gall-bladder problems, heart problems and cancer. This should be an indication that not only the additives used in food and water but other sources cause some of these problems.

In 1997 *Hardcopy* ran a special on arsenic-treated playgrounds. This is from what is known as CCA-treated pine wood, which is an arsenic-based treatment. High levels of arsenic have been detected on playground wood as well as the soil around it after a few years of weather exposure.

On March 26, 2001, the following article was published in a local newspaper:

WOOD LEAKS ARSENIC, STUDY SAYS

St. Petersburg, FL—A type of pressure-treated wood used to build several playgrounds, decks and picnic tables leaks arsenic at levels higher than state environmental officials consider safe, a newspaper's investigation found.

This wood, banned as environmentally hazardous in many countries, is sold in lumber stores across the United States. It is widely used in Florida because it stands up to termites, beetles and humidity.

The arsenic comes from chromated copper arsenate, a powerful pesticide injected into the wood that can leak into soil around it, the *St. Petersburg Times* reported Sunday based on a study from a laboratory hired by the newspaper.

Small doses of arsenic can be fatal, and long-term exposure can cause caner, but it is unclear whether contact with arsenic leaking from posts and boards is dangerous. Most home supply stores sell picnic tables made of the wood, even though wood-treatment companies say it should never be used for cutting or food preparation.

The laboratory conducted soil tests near the sunken posts at five wooden playgrounds. Every test detected levels of arsenic above the levels the state considers safe.

The wood industry says its studies show the wood is safe. The industry has fought efforts to ban CCA-treated lumber in Minnesota.

Switzerland, Vietnam and Indonesia have banned CCA-treated wood. Japan, Denmark, Sweden, Germany, Australia and New Zealand have restricted or proposed restriction for it. Connecticut health officials issued a warning three years ago that said children who frequently play on CCA-treated playgrounds come in contact with a major source of arsenic.

The Environmental Protection Agency banned most arsenic pesticides years ago but made an exception for pressure-treated wood.

These playgrounds were designed by the company and this treated wood was specified.

Their common method is to get several ladies in the community, who are educated and can get some publicity for organizing a group of volunteers for construction. Most are mothers, and it is unbelievable that they would subject their children to this deadly poison. Any level of arsenic is dangerous, and higher levels are fatal. Lower levels are suspected of causing cancer.

These playgrounds have been constructed all over the U.S.A., including some cities, counties, and some federal parks. State governments and federal officials should stop this immediately, and force the specifier to pay for cleanup of the site. Lately, the State of Florida has closed all playgrounds constructed with CCA-treated wood.

Also, some cities have traces of arsenic in water systems. These should be taken seriously because no one seems to know that level of contamination is acceptable. In my opinion no level of arsenic and chemical contaminations is acceptable.

We are reaching a critical level on waste disposal. The book, *The Waste Makers*, by Vance Packard, written many years ago is excellent reading on this subject.

Chapter VII

HISTORICAL PERSPECTIVE—EARLY 1900s

The following was taken from the writings of a lady who was born in 1907 in the Central United States.

In August a group of neighbors (eight or ten) would hire a fellow who had a steam engine that pulled a threshing machine. This machine separated oats, wheat from the shocks of straw. They had a binder that put the grain bundles together from rows that had been cut and raked into windrows. The binder picked up the straw and grain and bound them into bundles. A helper went behind it and put the bundles into shocks of about six bundles.

When the thresher came they loaded the shocks on wagons and hauled them to the threshing machine. All the neighbors helped each other at the threshing. In July red top hay was stacked.

In August after the grain was all threshed then they started back, changed sieves in the threshing machine and started back for the "run" to thresh the red top and separate the seed from the hay, and blew the hay into the barn or stacked it in the barn lot.

The women went to each other's homes to help cook for the threshers.

When the cold winters came later people had their straw and hay handy to feed.

My father taught school so he tried to get his threshing done before school started. Mother and I always found out whether the threshers were coming to our house the next day for dinner or not. If they were coming, the afternoon before when we got home from helping the neighbors cook, we churned cream for fresh butter and buttermilk. We caught and penned our fryers to dress, set yeast to make a fresh pan of light bread and buns for the next day's dinner.

We gathered vegetables from the garden and made fresh cheese from our clabber. The butter, cheese and milk were hung in the well in a large bucket with a rope tied to our pump.

We got corn roasting ears to fix, dressed our chickens, baked pies or cake. We usually had apple pie, coconut and blackberry. We also had pickles we had made from the garden earlier in the season.

We used a cook stove that burned wood. It heated the oven and also a water reservoir on the back of the stove. We always had hot water. Also we made iced tea and coffee.

The two men usually stayed all night.

For breakfast we usually had ham and eggs with biscuits and gravy. Also we had apple sauce or jelly of some kind with butter and coffee.

One year we had a fellow by the name of Filkill. He had an eighteen or nineteen-year-old boy to take care of the threshing machine and help feed wood to the engine to produce power for the threshing machine. They stayed all night and the next morning it was a little cool. We saw the boy standing close to the stove like he was cold. We thought maybe he was bashful. When we made up his bed we found out why he was cold. He was trying to dry his clothes. We had to wash the bedclothes too.

My uncle took rheumatic fever and was sick. The doctor told Grandpa to take him to California and thought that would help him. So Grandma and Grandpa took my father's brother to California.

Grandpa got a job at a livery stable where he took care of horses. We missed them so much and Grandpa went out behind his house and cried most every evening.

For Christmas Grandma, Grandpa and my uncle sent me a very pretty doll dresser with mirrors and drawers all covered with small white shiny shells. It was the most beautiful thing I had ever seen.

Grandma and Grandpa and my uncle stayed only one year till they came back home. My uncle got better and he could help around the place and could walk over to our house.

One summer I had a rail yard fence where I could crawl from the yard to the barn and I was at the barn playing and decided I would go back to the house for a drink. When I crawled through the yard fence I saw my father laying on the well porch. He had the prettiest red socks on and I wondered where he got them. He had a pillow under his head. I walked over and kissed him and he said, "Honey, I got hurt." Mother had called Grandma and the doctor.

A boar (male hog) got out of his pen. My father was chasing him to get the boar back into the pen. The boar turned on him and made a terrible gash in his leg. It was bleeding terrible. That was why his socks were red. If he hadn't had on tight underwear he probably would have bled to death.

About that time the doctor came with his pill bag. Grandma and Grandpa were there. They carried my father into the house and put him on the bed. They had nothing to put him asleep or numb the pain. The doctor pulled the artery ends together and tied them together with clamps. My father was trying to stand the pain but made terrible noises for it was hurting. I buried my head on Grandma's lap and cried too. Mother had to keep boiling water for the doctor to use. After the bleeding was stopped my father was easy but he had to stay in bed a week and was still weak when he began to sit up.

I and Mother took good care of him and I helped with the chores. I learned to milk a cow too. I enjoyed taking my father's meals to him. He was glad when he could sit at the table.

In the spring Grandpa got his nephew to help him get oats out of my father's granary to sow. Grandpa never could stand a mouse or bird twittering in his hands. As they scooped the oats into a sack his nephew found a nest of little mice. He slipped a little mouse into Grandpa's pocket. After they had filled their sack he asked Grandpa for a string to tie it with. Grandpa felt in his pocket and touched that mouse. I felt so sorry for him. I thought he would go into convulsions before he got it out. His nephew laughed and laughed and thought it was funny.

My father taught school about every winter so we usually went to town Saturday and to church on Sunday.

We had a nice church with about two and a half dozen people

and a preacher who preached every Sunday. He lived in the parsonage the church built for him. He had a girl about my age whom I liked very much.

I had the nicest Sunday school teacher. She was a very sweet woman. Her sister taught school too. They had a brother and their father died when the children were young. The "old" folks had an older teacher, who was also an elementary school teacher, and was our mail carrier also. It was a Presbyterian church where my mother's family went most of their lives. I was also christened there when I was about one year old.

My mother's maiden name was Benner. Grandma and Grandpa Benner moved to their home north of town when their oldest child, Ora, was small. They were married in Rinard, where they lived before moving north of town. I used to go with Grandma and Grandpa to Rinard to see Grandma's sister, Fanny, and her mother, my great-grandma.

As Grandpa's home north of town had to be made warmer they built a fireplace in their living room. They used wood heaters and had a large cook stove that also burned wood. In the fall they would cut a large wood pile and haul it to the barnyard, pile it up and a man with a wood saw would come and saw it into lengths that could be put in the heaters.

Grandpa's had a cellar built close to a well pump. They put a trough (concrete) through the cellar. In the trough they would run cold water and put their crocks of milk, also their butter and cheese. David and Martha always had a big garden, they had a grapevine in their garden and also grew garlic. They raised crops of corn, capricorn, oats, wheat on their cleared land. From their timber they had hickory nuts, walnuts, hazelnuts, and blackberries. They had a nice orchard too.

In the fall they would dig their potatoes, pick their apples and store them in the cellar. Then they would dig sweet potatoes, gather their late cabbage and store them in the cellar too. They put their sweet potatoes, beets and cabbage in boxes filled with dry sand. When they had turnips and radishes they would store them in the sand boxes. In the fall they always butchered four or five of their fattened hogs. When they trimmed the meat they rendered the fat into lard. They saved the cracklings to use in crackling corn bread. They used the lard for pies, cakes, bread loaves and to fry in. They salted the hams, shoulders, sides of the hogs with six cups of salt, one cup of pepper and one cup of brown sugar.

The meat stayed in this for two or three months. Then they would wash off the salt, hang it up in a meat house. They put a tub and put some ashes in the bottom, then put hickory wood on top of the ashes. They would start a fire on the hickory wood box, then they had to put water on the flame to make it smoke. It took about a week to smoke the joints and bacon properly.

The sausage was canned so it would not get old. Grandma would clean some of the hogs' intestines and put some sausage in it to smoke. She nearly always mixed some garlic buds ground in her sausage. I thought it tasted better with that as my folks never put garlic in their sausage.

Mother had a sister who married Jay Dow. Uncle Charley, a brother, married Jenny Webb.

Most every Christmas we would spend with Grandma Benner, one year Jay Dow's, one year Charley Benner's and the next year they would all be at our house.

The Dows had two children to play with, Marguerite and Roscoe. Uncle Charley had Frances so we all had a good time while the old folks visited.

Usually we spent Thanksgiving with my father's family or they would be at our house.

One Thanksgiving we had butchered a hog and were taking a shoulder of pork for them to use till they butchered later. There was a skiff of snow and my father had a wagon bed on a home-made wood sled he pulled with two horses. He put some hay in the bed and some covers to keep us warm. The edge of the sled caught in the end of the corduroy of wood the road commissioner had installed in a hole in the road. It turned the sled over and penned me under the wagon bed with the shoulder of meat on top of me. The horses stopped and Mother and Daddy lifted the wagon bed to let me out. I was unhurt, only had the breath knocked out of me for a while. Grandma and Grandpa always had a big jar of sauerkraut in their bedroom and it was delicious kraut. They always had a very good Thanksgiving dinner.

In the winter the roads were very muddy sometimes. I and our neighbor girl Youthel Berry walked one and a quarter mile to school.

One evening after it had rained all day we walked next to the fence to keep out of the mud. Our overshoes were slick from the wetness of the rain. Youthel slipped and stepped on the muddy road. She lost her overshoe. I pulled her back on the bank of the fence row. I proceeded to get her overshoe, pulled it out of the mud and lost my overshoe in the process. I pulled my overshoe out and got back on the bank and we went on home. We were a muddy mess though I know our mothers hated it but neither said anything to us.

The next winter my father taught Russell school. He had a one-horse cart and he took me to school with him. That winter Lash Hale had children who took the measles. They always quarantined people when they had the measles. They called and appointed my father to quarantine the Hales. As we went to school he proceeded to put up the quarantine. Lash Hale came out and called my father every name he could think of and threatened to shoot him if he put up that sign. Lash said he had sense enough to keep the kids at home and stay home himself till there was no danger. So my father drove me to school and took the sign back home with him. I was almost shaking with fear when I got to school.

The winter passed pretty fast. At Christmas time they locked my father out. He and I stood outside for two or three hours; finally my father said I treat, so they let him in. I was sure glad they had kept a good fire in the school house. It was good and warm.

When my father got his treat I got to help him sack it for the pupils. We set the treat in a box to take on Christmas Eve. That was fun. Then my father let me give each pupil an orange after they got their candy and peanuts. The next winter I went back to Center. We had double seats and always sat with someone.

In the summers I always had an old cat with a nest of kittens. I thought they were wonderful. I would take a ball tied to a string and the kittens would try to catch it with their paws. We had some nice times together. Sometimes I would wrap them in a blanket for a doll.

My grandma Smith thought cats' hairs made worms. She didn't like for me to play with the kittens so much.

One day she walked over to my house when I had company. We were in my playhouse in the orchard playing with our dolls. Grandma gathered up all my kittens and put them in a sack and proceeded to take them to the creek and drown them so I couldn't play with them. Pauline and I came back to the house to see her carrying the sack on her back, halfway down the road. Mother wouldn't let me go after her and when I found my kittens were gone I knew what she had done.

Anyway when I spent a week with Marguerite Dow or Frances Benner they always had some kittens to play with. Grandma Benner had some too. I always thought a lot of my grandparents, even if I thought they did me wrong I could forgive them.

We had neighbors about a quarter of a mile from our house, Mr. Forsythe. Their grandchildren would always come to my place to play with me or I could go play with them. We could play hide-and-seek, dare base or other games one couldn't play by themselves.

Mrs. Forsythe's father, Mr. Herdman, had a room at their house and he just loved for children to come in and talk to him. He always had a strip of candy filled with peanut butter, he gave each one that came to see him. Mrs. Forsythe had only one leg so she used crutches.

My husband's grandma and grandpa lived in the country and kept his farm producing. They had an ice house. It was built with two walls about four inches apart. Between these walls was filled with sawdust. Also the door was filled with sawdust. In the winter when the creek froze hard they would cut chunks of ice and put in the ice house. They had ice all summer the next summer. When we went to my grandpa's he would go get some ice and make ice cream. Everyone had cows for milk, eggs and sugar on hand with some vanilla or lemon flavoring. By fall they sold and used all their ice.

Most people grew sorghum cane. In the fall they would strip the cane, haul the stalks of cane to a mill.

At the cane mill they had a horse that went round and round

to grind the cane and run the juice into a trough that was heated by wood. They kept this juice boiling till it was thickened a bit. Then they caught it into five-gallon lard cans for the people to take home. We had sorghum all winter. With biscuits and butter it was delicious. Also we had some good gingerbread too. That went good for our school lunches. We always hilled up our potatoes, apples, beets and cabbage. We would make a pile of straw underneath the vegetables and fruit, cover them with straw and put dirt about six inches deep all around the hill. Then we put boards all around it to shed off the water.

In winter we made a hole in the hill to get out what we wanted then stuck a rag in the hole and covered it with a board.

We dug wells, and got very good water. If they were twenty or thirty feet deep it was usually good soft water but if you went one hundred or more feet you were apt to get good water but it was "hard" water full of minerals.

As far as purity was concerned it was pure. We hadn't used fertilizers, insecticide or such. Barn yard and chicken manure was used and that was all we had. We had extra good gardens and fair crops. 100 bu. corn or 30 bu. oats and wheat. We had enough to feed that livestock we had and our chickens.

Almost everyone had an orchard usually apples, peaches, pears, cherries, grapes and a patch of strawberries in their gardens. Also asparagus and rhubarb were there too. In the timbers were hickory nuts, walnuts, hazelnuts. Also the creeks any size had fish you could fish and get a mess of fish anytime.

I used to go with Grandma and Grandpa and my uncle to Grandma's sisters that lived north of Farina. They had a strawberry patch of about forty acres. They always hired about twenty-five strawberry pickers. There were always people who want to make a little money for they could pick about fifty quarts a day and they were paid three cents per quart. Some could pick one hundred quarts.

There would always be a lot of children there to play with. We played Blackman hide-and-seek, dare base, drop the handkerchief. Mrs. Burkett always made a large strawberry shortcake, enough to feed the pickers and all the company they had. She always had garden vegetables and huge amounts of chicken or a goose roasted. She always had whipped cream to go with the shortcake too.

Also I would go with Grandma and Grandpa to Grandpa's half-sisters who lived in Flora. They had children too for me to play with while the old folks visited.

Grandpa had a surrey with two seats and a fringed top and it was pulled by two horses.

They used to have a fair in Flora and my father and mother would fix a picnic lunch with iced tea to drink to take with us and we would drive the horse and buggy to the fair. I had a little seat I put in the bottom of the buggy between my father and mother.

They always had a horse race and I could ride on the merry-go-round for ten cents a ride.

They also had funny clowns running around throwing out peanuts. When it came time to eat we would get a good shady spot, spread down our tablecloth and have fried chicken, potato salad, sliced tomatoes and some kind of cookies or cake.

Also my folks would go to Flora to see my father's cousin. Her husband worked in the round house in Flora as train inspector. She nearly always had steak and mashed potatoes with sliced tomatoes with some boughten cookies and fruit salad; it was rare for us to have steak.

We kept cattle but kept them for milk, butter and cheese and sold one or two a year to get money for other things we needed.

We kept hogs for our meat with the chickens we raised for fryers. We always butchered three fattened hogs and cured and smoked the meat. Mother always kept a ham to use during the strawberry season.

I had long curls until I was about eight years old then my mother combed it and braided it in two braids.

One Christmas I wanted a wide red ribbon for my hair so Mother got me one for Christmas. I was anxious to find out what she got so I snooped around and found it where she hid it. I was overjoyed to know I was getting a nice wide ribbon. I didn't intend to tell Mother I had found it but one day we were talking and I told her how pretty the ribbon was. She knew I had found it. "Alright," she said, "I will just give that ribbon to your cousin." I was so sorry I had told her and cried about it.

Later I found out that Grandma had bought me a nice ribbon. I was proud of it at Christmas time but it wasn't quite as wide as I really wanted.

Mother got me a nice warm stocking cap with a scarf built on it and a tassel on the end. I was real proud of that cap so my mother was forgiven and everything was alright.

I usually stayed a week at Aunt Effie and Marguerite's in the summer. Uncle Jay and Roscoe were usually busy in the field.

Marguerite and I had never dressed a chicken but we decided we would try it. We put water on the stove to heat as we had to put more wood in the stove too.

Then we proceeded to catch a chicken. We chased and chased and decided to get some of them in the hen house. So we cornered off about four or five and guided them to the henhouse and got them inside.

We got in and locked the door so it wasn't long till we had our chicken. By that time the water was boiling on the stove. Marguerite couldn't wring the chickens head off so I took it and put my foot on its head and yanked it off the chicken. We got our hot water in a bucket and doused the chicken in the hot water to get the feathers loose. We picked the feathers off the chicken, then got a pan of cold water to wash it and get the pin feathers off the chicken. We threw that out and got some fresh cold water and proceeded to cut it up. We had seen our mothers do it so we pretty well knew how to do it.

We cut it up, took it in the house, put the grease in a skillet to fry it in. We salted and peppered it and rolled it in flour then put it in the skillet.

Aunt Effie had us to pick her peas in the garden that morning and we had hulled them ready to cook. We went to the garden and got some young potatoes from the hills and took them and washed them and scraped them. Then we cooked the peas and potatoes together.

When the chicken was done we made good chicken gravy. Aunt Effie, Uncle Jay and Roscoe thought they had a delicious dinner. We were quite proud of our accomplishment of getting a dinner ready by ourselves.

By this time my uncle was married and had built himself a

house about a quarter of a mile from Grandpa's.

When I would go to Grandpa's to stay a few days I would always go see my uncle and aunt. I helped Grandpa pull the worms off his tobacco while he hoed his potatoes.

When I went to stay a week with my other grandma and grandpa, Grandma would let me help her hunt turkey nests and help her fix boards up to her celery to bleach it. She didn't let me hoe anywhere only where weeds grew alongside the garden. Mother always let me hoe some. I had a little hoe. At night Grandpa wanted me to play flinch with him. It would tickle him if he got to flinch me. I tried not to let him.

Usually some time during the week Marguerite or Frances would come over to play with me.

Also Grandma had a neighbor who had a little girl who had been burned badly from an outside fire when they were roasting corn. Grandma and I would go over to see her in the afternoon. Her name was Brown.

When I was about eight years old I learned that one of my mother's sisters had gone to the state of Washington to work in an uncle's clothing store.

I also had an uncle who went to Idaho to take up a claim on eighty acres. The land there was just being settled. His place was about forty miles from Boise, Idaho. He always went down to the valley from there and picked apples. He built himself a house to live in but never married.

When my grandpa Benner got sick I went to stay with Grandma to help her with her work. Grandpa was sick most of the summer and died that fall. Of course I went to school that winter and Grandma moved back to her home. She had moved closer to town when Grandpa got sick so the doctor could get out to see him. I could see Grandma was so lonesome and needed someone to be with her. I was writing to my uncle so in the spring I wrote to him to come live with Grandma.

He came to take care of the cattle, hogs and the farm for half of the profits. Grandma kept her chickens for grocery money and saved some too. At that time grain was cheap so it didn't take much to feed the chickens, horses and cattle, and hogs.

Aunt Clara and their son Wilbur came to our house for

Grandpa's death. We met her at the train. Wilbur was a little older than me. We looked at pictures and got him acquainted with the farm and farm animals as he had always lived in town. I had a play house under the apple tree. We got some clay mud and made dishes to put out in the sun to dry.

It was lonesome when they went home.

I had a baby sister to play with. She had been born a year before that. One night my father and mother woke me up and ask me if I wanted to go to Grandpa's. Of course I always wanted to go to Grandpa's.

Grandma Smith's mother had died and she was to be buried the next day. My father said he couldn't go to the funeral so I could go with Grandpa.

The next morning my parents called and said they had a nice baby girl. I couldn't wait to get home and see her so Grandpa took me back home. We named my sister Bernice Alma. I thought that was a pretty name and I was so proud of her. Now I could have some company!

I went to my great Grandma's funeral with Grandpa too.

When my sister was about three years old I went after the cows at the crossroads north of our house where my father had a pasture. I decided to take my sister with me and she wanted to go. We arrived at the crossroads and started to look for the cows as there were low hickory brush growing and the cows could hide. My sister got tired so I picked her up, put her on my back and went ahead.

I heard a peculiar weird sound that sounded like some kind of animal. It scared me but I didn't let my sister know I was scared. I looked on the bushes and saw a bat. I had never seen one before but I didn't see how so small an animal could make such a weird sound.

We found the cows and took them home. We ran most of the way. When I got home and told my father about it, he laughed and said that was some children playing with the whistle of the threshing machine that was at the neighbors. After he got his work done he went to the machine to help service the separator as it would be at our house the next day. I learned after that not to suspect such a small animal to make such a big noise.

When I graduated from the grades we had to write on a final examination covering the whole eight grades. Several came to Center, my home school. We were playing drop the handkerchief at the noon hour after our lunch. We had a very bashful boy. One of the girls, as she was going to drop the handkerchief, lost her dress skirt. It hit and of course her slip was showing. Everyone began to laugh and she picked it up and threw it at the bashful boy. His face got red and I thought he was going to faint. After she dropped the handkerchief she picked up her skirt, put it on and I saw she had lost her buttons. I had a safety pin I gave her to fasten her skirt up. All was back to normal again.

I passed the grades with a good grade then I was ready for high school.

That summer Grandma bought a new car. My father had bought one the fall before. Grandma wanted to go to see their son who had gone to Nekoosa, Wisconsin, several years before to work in the paper factory. She wanted Marguerite to go with her daddy to drive. She wanted me to go too, so the folks let me.

The first evening we got to Rockford, IL. We spread our blankets down along the road and slept that night. The next morning we ate a sandwich Grandma had fixed and then we started on to Wisconsin.

The next night we were just north of Illinois in southern Wisconsin. That was the farthest away from home I had ever been and so many sights to see. Everyone was amazed at the large cities and beautiful country. It was in August and the trees were so pretty. We slept in Wisconsin for the first time.

The next day we arrived in Nekoosa at Uncle Charley's house. They all came out to greet us and all tried to talk at once. When Uncle Charley came home that night he welcomed us all with a hug and kiss. He had plans for us all week. Grandma enjoyed visiting with Aunt Jenny. I think the first few days she was tired and enjoyed her rest.

Uncle Charley had a dairy and a large cucumber patch.

The oldest girl, Frances, could drive a truck (pickup).

The cucumbers had to be picked every other morning. The children, Frances, Harold, Donald and Mildred, picked the pickles for spending money. When we all picked cucumbers, we,

Frances, Marguerite and I hauled them to the pickle factory.

Frances took us to the Dells one day to see the dance pavilion. We had never seen one before as we didn't have them around in Southern Illinois.

One day we went picnicking on the river and also went swimming and boat riding.

Grandma thought the battery of her car was low so she ordered another battery from Sears Roebuck in Chicago. It usually took three days to get an order from Sears. We were having such a good time that when the battery came we hid it.

One night Frances had a date with a boyfriend. Harold, Donald, Marguerite and I fixed up some dummy characters and stuffed them with straw and placed them where her boyfriend drove up when they came home. We hid to see what they had to say. When they came home Frances told her boyfriend he must walk her to the door, she was afraid to go by herself. We could hardly keep from laughing at her but we didn't dare laugh. When we came into the house she knew who did it. We all had a big laugh.

Uncle Charley took us through the paper factory. There were people they hired to cut the logs from the northern pine. They cut them as long as possible. Then they put them on the river and floated them down to the paper mill. Men stood on the logs with long probes and kept them floating. The machinery at the factory had jaws that sawed the logs into small chunks and picked the wood into small bits almost looked like sawdust.

This wood went into a large vat where acid turned the pieces into a liquid. This liquid ran through a trough to another vat that cooked the pulp until it was thick and chemicals were in the vat to turn the liquid into paper material.

Then it went to the rollers that rolled it into wrapping paper and cardboard box material.

They made the boxes all sizes by hand and had clamps to clamp them together. Wrapping paper was in large rolls. These were shipped from the factory in flattened boxes and rolls of paper. Stores bought the paper and put the boxes together. Everything was shipped by train in those days.

I had belonged to the 4 H Club that summer and had a gilt for my project. Grandma Benner had loaned me twenty-five dollars for me to buy a gilt that spring. I fed it and got a nice spotted gilt ready for the fair that fall before I went to Wisconsin. I showed the gilt and got first prize on it and second prize on my record book.

I had to wash with ivory soap suds and rinse the gilt with clear water to make its hair look shiny. I put some grease on it. There were several in our club.

Flora had purchased the Brown land and donated it for a fair ground. They had stalls for our livestock and we each took care of our show animals.

I also had white rock chickens for a project too. That summer our farm advisor came to our club meetings and showed us how to caponize chickens and how to care for our other projects.

At the fair I showed a pen of one rooster, two hens, a pen of two pullets and a capon pen of three capons. I got first on my rooster and two hens and third on my capon, second on my pen of pullets.

That helped me to have some money to pay Grandma her twenty-five dollars and have some spending money.

We had to wash the feathers of all the chickens to make their feathers snowy white and fluffy.

When I went to high school we had a class of nineteen freshmen. I became acquainted with a lot of children at high school. We had good teachers and a good principal. I was not a good student in arithmetic in the grades. After I took algebra my arithmetic opened up like a book. I never had any more trouble with arithmetic. In my grammar class we had Miss Hackett for our teacher. Mr. Smith liked to spout off and get the class laughing. When he didn't want to study he would try to entertain the teacher and class so they didn't find out he hadn't studied his lesson. The winter was bad so I got a room to stay in, which was upstairs. I studied about every night except prayer meeting night when we went to church. One of the high school girls rang the bell. She liked for me to help her ring the bell and get ready for prayer meeting.

I usually went home on weekends. I was getting tired of long hair and most girls were bobbing their hair. I felt out of place with long braided hair. I asked my father if I could cut my hair. He first said, "No," but my mother said she didn't care so I finally persuaded my daddy to say if nothing else would do me I might cut it.

When I went back to my room I thought he might call back and tell me not to cut it so I went to a girlfriend's house and told her to cut it off. She and her mother were pretty good barbers so they bobbed it for me. I was proud of it. Sure enough the next morning my father called me up and told me I'd better not have my hair cut. I told him it was already done. That was the last I heard of that.

That winter they were building a paved road on Route 50. They were having a program at the high school they called the Lyceum. A friend and I were walking along the street and we met a couple of boys and asked them to buy Lyceum tickets. One boy told her he would buy two if she would go with him. Another said he would buy two tickets if I would go with him. So we sold four tickets. When the evening came the boys came together and picked us up and took us to the Lyceum. We enjoyed the program very much. We went home and I didn't want a boyfriend so when he asked for another date I refused but my friend went with her date again and finally married him.

My second year of high school my folks moved to town. My father taught the 8th grade. I made good grades and my third year they let me teach the 3rd grade when the teacher was sick.

I always admired my teachers and admired my father and mother when my first year of school I went to school to both of them.

I graduated with seventeen of the nineteen who had started. Two dropped out of high school. I had to write for a teacher's certificate then go to college a summer after I taught. I went to Louisville to take my examination. Several others were there too.

I passed with good grades so next I must locate a school. I succeeded in getting a country school at Fairview, south of Iola. I had twenty-eight pupils enrolled. That summer I went with my first boyfriend who taught me to drive his Ford touring car. Finally I let a friend have him and I bought myself a Ford roadster to drive to my school, for $325. The same day I got my Ford my father bought a new Chevrolet touring car for $495.

I drove to my school as long as the roads weren't too muddy, then I stayed with an uncle close to the school. Another friend, who would be my future brother-in-law, had gone to Carbondale to get his teaching certificate, and taught the first district south of mine. I would wait on Saturday until he made a track in the mud, then I would follow it to the end of our lane. Sometimes I would get stuck before I got home, so it was time for me to stay at my uncle's house. There were lots of young people in the neighborhood.

One Saturday evening two young men came by and wanted me and a friend to attend the "show" at a nearby town. We went and as we went under the railroad trestle we got stuck in the mud. I drove their car and the boys pushed and we went on to the movie. It was a good movie at the theater. There was a small hamburger stand in Louisville so they took us and got us a hamburger and Coke. We got home early so Bessie stayed all night with me. Uncle Will and Wilma enjoyed it very much for our company.

When it snowed the boys would put a wagon bed on a wooden sled and fill the wagon bed floor with straw or hay. They would gather all the young people in the neighborhood and take them for a sleigh ride.

I enjoyed my school teaching and when it came time for Christmas I went to school one morning and they had locked me out. They had built the fire in the stove in the school house so they were warm. They wanted me to say treat. I fooled around with them until 9:30 then I jumped in my car and went to Iola and got enough chewing gum for all the pupils. When I went back I said, "Treat." They let me in and I gave each a stick of chewing gum. I let them take their seats and chew the gum till recess time that was 10:30. By that time they were ready to study for the rest of the day. We had a Christmas program. Children sang songs and we had a Christmas play they acted out and a nice crowd came to help them enjoy Christmas. We drew names for presents and I had sacks of treats and an orange for them.

In the spring we had a pie supper. We had an auctioneer of some person in the district. Each girl brought a pie. We had a cake for the most popular girl, a bar of soap for the man with the dirtiest feet, a pair of socks for the man with the biggest feet and a jar of sweet pickles for the most lovesick couple.

We cleared about ninety dollars to buy reading circle books for our library and exam paper for our exams.

I had a sow and pig project the next summer. I went to Charleston College for six weeks, then came home to finish my project for 4H and set out a strawberry patch before I went to college. I had time to hoe it after I came home.

The college was quite different from high school. Two friends went with me for they had taught one year of school also.

I showed my sow and pigs at the fair in August and got third prize.

My father mulched my strawberries for me one Saturday after school had started. He taught in the winter too. My second term was at Dayton as it was close enough to drive back and forth, then when the roads got bad I could ride a horse. I had a nice school and neighborhood to work in; another lady taught at the district south of mine. My oldest son later married the daughter of this lady. The people of both districts were good friends and very cooperative. We had a nice program for Christmas, and some older young people came to help in our programs. After our program, we went to the adjoining district to see their program.

We had a pie supper too and netted us around eighty-nine dollars with which to buy library books, exam paper and chalk for the blackboard.

Mrs. Humphry lived on the corner of the road that led to school. She quilted quilts for extra money. I had pieced three quilts in my spare time so I got the material for the lining and got my filling and had her to quilt them. She did a nice job.

I went to work at the shoe factory in the neighboring town. Wreatha went with me. We worked six weeks to get enough money to go back to college for six weeks. We boarded at Mrs. Vaughn's.

After six weeks at the factory we went back to college. We stayed at Mr. Anderson's again. We enjoyed our classes and our evenings were spent studying. My father was going to college too so it was hot in his room and he would come study with us in the evenings.

My next school was Forest Grove. People tried to warn me it was a rough district to teach in. I sort of dreaded to begin for I didn't know what to expect. I had a large school but seemed to get along fine with the children.

We had a wiener roast at Halloween. Everyone seemed to have a good time but I found a few greedy people who filled their pockets too. At Christmas time we had a nice program and all seemed to be happy. I had a little boy named Vernon. He had an older brother who brought him to school when the weather was nice.

I had a room at a neighbor's house where I batched. I could walk to school after the roads were bad. I enjoyed walking while the weather was nice. Vernon always walked. He could entertain us as they took the *Globe Democrat* and he could tell us about the funnies and what the characters did and said. At our wiener roast I saw his older brother and got acquainted with him. He brought his cousin with him and picked me up to go along and she put me in the middle. I couldn't see why she did that as I thought she was his girlfriend.

At the pie supper he was there and one of the girls gave him her number for she wanted to eat pie with him. As it happened he didn't get her pie after all. I went home with him after the pie supper. I had come to like him very much.

We had a nice Christmas program and all seemed to go smoothly. When school was out a big dinner was brought by the patrons and enjoyed by all it seemed. That spring we three girls were back to college. I sold my hogs and the folks bought a piano. I had learned to play an organ but the piano was a lot better to practice on.

We finished our eighteen weeks at college and had a nice vacation at home. While at college we would finish our classes at 3:30 P.M. It was still hot so we would all get in my roadster and would go to the lake swimming. By the time we got back it had cooled off enough we could study and eat our supper.

One night we were in our room seeing who could do the most exciting exercises. I guess we were talking too loud and were enjoying it so much. One of the girls was touching her toes with her fingers and laughing. Something told us to look up and there was the landlady standing in our door laughing. She had heard us and came to see what it was all about. We were quieter after that.

Of the two girls who stayed across the hall from us, one was a married lady and the other was still single. They went out walking about every night. I think they ate their suppers at a restaurant not far from there. We always brought enough from home for our meals.

One weekend at Decoration time three boys met up with us in a pickup loaded with peonies. They had a red peony and passed us as they passed they threw a red peony to the driver and that was me. We passed them and they threw two white peonies to our car and said it was for the other two. They followed us to Mattoon where we turned off to go back to college. They wrote their names on a piece of paper and threw it to us. They were three boys going back to a nearby town to work. At college we had a psychology teacher who would slam a book on the desk then watch to see how many jumped at the noise. That would be his theme for the lesson. Sometimes he would yawn and see how many did that or would cough or sneeze then watch the class to see how many did that too.

My folks sold everything they had around the farm and bought a house in town. My father taught in the 8th grade and my brother and sister were ready for high school. That was the fall of 1928.

I got a school to teach just north of Flora. The school house sat where the water plant is now. That was 1929–30.

My future husband went to Chicago that spring to get a job and see his sister. He didn't get a job and came back to Sharpsburg where he shucked corn.

That summer he and his brother came back home where he farmed his father's farm.

One Sunday they came after me to go to the show at a small theater. He had his cousin and I had to go with his brother. He had gotten into a bees' nest and one stung him below the eye. His cheek was all swelled up.

We went to the show and enjoyed it very much. They took me home first so their cousin was taken home as they went.

That fall when my folks had their sale he was at the sale. He asked me about Mother's hens. I talked to him for a while.

I taught at Lacey school south of Farina. I stayed with a local family. I had a few boyfriends that winter but didn't care for any of them. The landlady was a good cook but I went home about every weekend I could.

At Thanksgiving I had to go on the train from Farina to Edgewood, then catch a train going to Flora. When I got to Edgewood the train had already gone south so I had to get a taxi. I paid $8 for a taxi to Flora. My future husband was supposed to meet me there, but he didn't come. I was terribly disappointed so I called my boyfriend at Farina to come. He came and we traveled on the paved road to Bluford where his sister lived. We ate supper there with his sister and husband. Then we went on to Salem and Alma, Kinmundy and back to Farina to my school.

Everything went smoothly. I had a little boy who seemed not to be able to learn to read and get his numbers. I got some cigar boxes and a coping saw and some glue. I taught him to make doll furniture. We also used empty spools. Then I made paper money and taught him the value of $1,50 cents, 25 cents, 10 cents and 5 cents.

He would sell his doll furniture to the other children for so much money. He learned to write his name too. It kept me working every day and at night too. At Christmas he made ornaments for the Christmas tree and sold them to the other children.

The rest of the school children were very good. They enjoyed their pie supper, Christmas program and were good to study and made good grades.

In later life I have seen the children grow up and all seem to be doing alright. My little boy grew up and had a cabinet shop and sold and fixed furniture. He married a nice wife who helped him in his work. Then they moved out of state and have some business there and are raising a nice family.

That spring I went home and helped my mother clean house. My future husband came to see me a time or two there. Then I went to help Grandma Benner clean house. My boyfriend was there every evening after his field work was done for the day. He had seven cows to milk. He asked me to marry him so I thought about it and finally accepted. He ordered my ring after I picked it out and made plans for a May 17 wedding. My grandmother was overjoyed for she had known his mother's sister who had lived as neighbors to Grandma. She gave me her blessings and wished us a long happy life.

On May 17 he finished planting one hundred acres of corn with horses.

My folks set out sweet potato plants that morning and I helped. Then Mother and I went to town to get my wedding dress and some meat for supper. She was going to get supper for us.

When we got home my future husband was there talking to my sister. We went to Louisville to be married at the parsonage of the Methodist preacher. He had to go back home after his mother so I waited at his uncle's house. When he came back with his mother he brought the preacher and we were married at his uncle's house. He wasn't twenty-one yet so he had to have his mother's consent for him to marry.

When we got back to Flora it was raining. We ate supper then went home to his folks.

As we were about home we had a flat tire on our car. He got out in the mud to take the tire off, then we went in on the rim. The next morning we fixed the tire.

I had sold my roadster as I had about worn it out.

I taught two schools when I found out we were going to have a baby. Then we moved to a farm after school was out. My husband's brother and his wife had parted and he brought his two children who were two and four years old. My husband's mother wasn't able to look after both of them so we took one of them to be with us. On October 11 we had a baby boy. His father wanted him named after his grandfather. That fall his nephew would take his lunch to school and I usually had cookies or cake with fruit for dessert. A little neighbor boy who went to the same school would stop for him. He never had dessert so I would put some cookies or fruit in his lunch bucket. He liked it very much. A few days after we got our son, his nephew's mother came to get her boys. She had gone to Terre Haute, where her daughters could go to school and was baking pies to sell the factory workers so she could support the boys.

My mother stayed a week with me after our son was born. At that time my husband had a truck and was hauling peaches, apples north making about $60 every two days. Also he bought watermelons and sold them that summer.

Seed buyers would call at the farms and test the seed for purity. They made a bid on what they could pay. Whichever buyer bid the most they would haul the grain sacks to an elevator or seed house. They would weigh it and pay the farmer so much per pound.

My husband's grandfather threshed for neighbors and friends for two or three cents per bushel.

In about 1938 my husband introduced tractors, 10-20 International, to be used instead of horses. People thought the wheels would make the ground so hard it wouldn't grow any crops.

After he farmed with tractors a year or two and raised better crops than he had with horses people began to get tractors to farm with. Gradually more farmers tried tractors. Some held on to their horses. Gradually tractors, larger plows, disc planters and combines were used. Rubber tired tractors were tried and they found they could raise better crops and more of the land became farmed.

The Small Town Description

At the beginning of the 1900s Xenia was a very efficient town. In the upper town at what is now Route 50 was an evaporator. They bought apples to make juice and dried apples. They put the apple juice in barrels and the dried apples were put in crates. Most of it was used by the local people. Some were shipped by railroad to the cities.

Across the road was a restaurant where the workers could eat their lunches if they didn't carry their lunches with them.

Across the road was a stone house that at one time was used for stage stop and rooms to stay in for transients. Downtown Mr. Beard had a hearse to transport the dead to the graveyard.

On down the street was a school house made of brick where the grades were on the first floor and high school on the second floor. They had three years' high school. The fourth year could be had by going to Flora. Also after graduating from Xenia we could write for an examination to get a teacher's certificate.

On down the street was the Methodist church and west of it was a Baptist church. The Christian church was built later south of the railroad.

On main street they began to gravel the road and later oiled the street to keep down the dust. It was in the 1920s that it was concreted after Route 50 was made.

On the first stop was a hardware store. Across the street was a jail house where criminals were held till they were taken to Louisville jail.

There was a feed and seed store where they sold all kinds of feed and seed to the farmers.

Next was a drugstore where people bought their medicines and toiletries. Dr. Fatheree had a doctor's office where he took care of the sick. Sometimes he traveled into the country to take care of patients.

Tig Tully had a store where he kept dry goods, groceries and bought eggs. They sold material for dresses, aprons, sheets, pillow slips, buttons, sewing thread and other underwear needed.

There were the Orchard City Bank, the Kroger grocery store and the Post Office, the Xenia State Bank and a stairway that lead upstairs where the telephone operator took care of the switchboard to help people call different places.

This store kept all kinds of dry goods, groceries, shoes and boots and bought eggs. They also sold dishes and across the road was another grocery store.

There was a railroad station along the railroad that signaled trains. People boarded cars to travel different places and mail was unloaded. Eggs were shipped to other cities. The farmers would ship corn by the ordering a carload when they had a crop failure. When the corn came in they would unload it into wagons and haul it home with horses. They needed to have corn to feed their horses, chickens and hogs.

Across the railroad station was Lyman Bryan's doctor's office. He also doctored at his office or traveled to the country homes.

Later this building became a garage. Harrison Gibson kept a

coal business where people bought coal to use for heating homes and stores, and also to feed some to hogs for mineral.

They had a blacksmith who repaired all kinds of harness, wagons, buggies and put shoes on horses. The shoes put on them were metal horseshoes nailed to the bottom of their feet and had cleats on them to prevent the horses from slipping on icy ground.

In the country north of Xenia was a small store kept by Mr. Beard. People could get some groceries without going to Xenia to trade.

Almost every farm had a small orchard of apples, peaches, plums, cherries and pears. They also had grapevines, rhubarb and large gardens that they raised for vegetables.

We could not buy bread but we could get corn ground for meal at a mill. We could also have wheat ground for bread. We could buy flour in twenty-five to fifty-pound sacks to bake light bread. We used hops to make yeast for bread.

Chapter VIII

MID AND LATE 1900s

All during this period from 1907 through to the early thirties, people seldom locked their doors to homes and the attitudes were "treat your neighbor as you wish to be treated". There were very few mind-altering drugs used. Most people were hard workers, good family-oriented people, and families would get together often.

After the great depression of 1929, many heavy investors in the stock market were considered wealthy, but lost everything they had almost overnight, and, as a result, some committed suicide, and some had to be admitted to mental facilities.

Many men would walk up to ten miles each way to work at a job for about fifty cents per day. The rural people made out better then their urban friends, because they could grow most of their food, and sold eggs, cream, and livestock to purchase other necessities. Cigarettes were ten cents per pack, gasoline was eleven to twelve cents per gallon, kerosene used in lamps was eight to nine cents per gallon, chewing gum was a penny a pack, eight-ounce soft drinks were a nickel per bottle. There was a surplus of repossessed autos in the cities, that could be purchased for thirty-five to seventy dollars. Most were one to three years old, with very low miles. Other commodities could be purchased at similar prices. Federal programs were initiated, such as WPA to build roads, and other projects, CCC which was the Civilian Conservation Corps to work on national parks, and similar projects, to employ the mass of men without work.

Wages were low, unemployment was high, and anyone living near a railroad had what were called "bums" or "hobos" who traveled the railroad on freight trains, and would go to nearby homes and beg for food. Most residents fed them on the porch or a table in the yard, and they had no trouble with them.

Communication was by battery-powered radios, and telephones that must go through a local operator for other lines or long distance. This was done manually and personally. The operators knew everyone in the community, and knew more about what was going on in the community than anyone else, because they had to listen to all calls. The men on their line were responsible for keeping their telephone lines in good working order.

Lighting was with kerosene lamps and lanterns. The Aladdin lamp was the greatest advancement thus far. It emitted much more light than its predecessor. Also during this period white gas was used, which greatly improved the light emitted.

Cities had electricity earlier, but most rural communities did not receive it until the mid-thirties through the Rural Electrification Agency (REA). The Tennessee Valley Authority (TVA) was organized to provide power to the southeast U.S.A. These paved the way for water pumps to pump water. And eventually the hot water heater, hot and cold running water, and bathrooms. Other areas of the U.S.A. had similar developments, paving the way for today's massive dependence on electricity. Heating was with wood or coal stoves, and cooking with what was known as "cook stoves".

When World War II erupted all able-bodied men were drafted for military service. Many items were rationed and subject to ceiling prices. Rationed items included tires, coffee, sugar, gasoline and everything of strategic importance. New autos and trucks were not available from 1942 until 1946. Farm equipment was only available with a permit. Price controls were established on many used items, including autos, farm equipment, airplanes, trucks, shop equipment and almost everything that could be purchased, because new items were not available. The "black market" flourished with only cash transactions, and on items that did not require a title. For example, an auto could only be sold for the ceiling price, but loose parts could be sold for any price. There were many high-priced tire jacks, spare tires, etc. sold, with auto and truck auctions all over the country. Honey was used as a sweetener replacing sugar in making ice cream, and other alternatives were used in other industries needing sweeteners.

Women were left to work in all factories and performed jobs previously reserved for men. They made ships, tanks, ammunition, and everything of strategic importance. All scrap metal was gathered up and sold for reuse in new materials.

The servicemen came from every line of work. They were innovative and worked as teams, never faltered, and did their best. Women volunteered as nurses and clerical positions.

After the surprise bombing of Pearl Harbor, on the morning of December 7, 1941, the U.S.A. was not prepared. Most of our ships and airplanes in the area were destroyed, and we were unable to respond adequately. We had one aircraft carrier in the Pacific, and it would change positions at night to make the Japanese think there were more. Many people were not aware how unprepared we were. Shipbuilders, aircraft factories, ammunition plants, clothing plants, vehicle factories and others went on twenty-four-hour days, seven-day schedules. One shipbuilder, Henry J. Kaiser, produced what was called "Liberty Ships" at an unprecedented rate. The merchant marine was integrated into the navy, and all cruise ships were to transport personnel, equipment, and supplies. Several did not make it and were sunk by enemy ships, airplanes, and mines in the water. All the servicemen didn't have time nor the desire for mind-altering and/or illegal drugs that plague our country now.

After World War II, those surviving came back, some with foreign brides, went to school/college on the G.I. Bill of Rights and were hard workers in their professions.

The book, *The Greatest Generation*, by Tom Brokaw is excellent reading on this subject.

Many returned with battle scars and injuries that were painful, but they endured and gave life in the U.S. their best. The same goes for prisoners of war, who suffered torture in the hands of their captors. The torture of POWs by the Germans was not so severe as those inflicted by Japan. However, these brave men were and are the proudest to be American. Many still won't talk about their ordeals, but a few are not bothered by their experiences and talk freely about them.

In 1946, new automobiles were then available. Some parts were molded from scrap metal. One, which was damaged, had the imprint of "Coca Cola" in the metal of the roof. Another, in a crash, the top opened up in the center, leaving a gaping hole in the roof.

The fifties were marred by the Korean War. This was the turning point where wars were called by other titles, i.e. police action, country assistance, etc.

This was more of a political war, initially between North and South Korea. The operation was very different than World War II. In Korea, standard uniforms were not used, and the Americans couldn't tell exactly who or where the "enemy" was. In other words it was more of a guerilla warfare with no set battle lines, no centralized battle area. The field commanders were professional and commanded their troops well. The draft was used which caused many young men to enlist in the service of their choice rather than be drafted. One of these, a man of draft age, tried to enlist in the navy, air force and army. He was turned down by these services, because of flat feet, drafted, and assigned to the Marine Corps. Needless to say he is not a "gung-ho" marine advocate.

This was the first war that met with resistance among some groups, and some young men escaped to Canada to evade the draft. There was no rationing or price controls as in World War II. The economy was progressing at a reasonable pace in the 1950s. In 1950, you could buy a new full size auto (Chev, Ford, Plymouth) for $1,300 to $1,600. We still had rural schools that functioned well and all the consolidations had not yet taken hold.

In the 1960s technology started to increase. NASA had already made good strides with the defection of a well-known PhD who escaped from Germany and brought several top notch engineers with him. This individual was responsible for the growth and accomplishments of NASA. We should not forget the Atomic Energy Commission for their development of nuclear power.

However, the war in Vietnam erupted and everything started to fall apart. Many demonstrations were against the war and increasing groups of people expressed their viewpoints through violence.

The Vietnam War was completely guerilla warfare, and impossible to determine who the enemy was. It may be a child of eight or nine years, an elderly lady, or anyone who may drop a grenade in your pocket at any time. Some field commanders stated that their threat from within was greater than from the Viet Cong, connected with mind-altering drug usage and dealing.

Most can remember what has happened since the Vietnam War. Great changes, not all of them for the better. We will discuss that in the next chapter, "The Beginning of the Twenty-First Century".

The following is a summary, Take a Walk With Me... Down Memory Lane, which came off the Internet. If you are old enough... take a stroll with me... close your eyes and go back before the Internet... before semiautomatics and crack... before SEGA or Super Nintendo... way back.

I'm talking about hide and go seek at dusk. Sitting on the porch, Simon Says. Kick the Can, Red Light – Green light. Lunch boxes with a thermos, chocolate milk, going home for lunch, penny candy from the store, hopscotch, butterscotch, skates with keys, Jacks, Mother May I? hula hoops and sunflower seeds, whist and Old Maid and Crazy Eights, wax lips and mustaches, Mary Janes, saddle shoes and Coke bottles with the names of cities on the bottom, running through the sprinkler, circle pins, bobby pins, Mickey Mouse Club, Rocky and Bullwinkle, Fran and Ollie, Spin and Marty... all in black and white. When around the corner seemed far away, and going downtown seemed like going some- where. Bedtime, climbing trees, making forts... backyard shows, lemonade stands, cops and robbers, cowboys and Indians, sitting on the curb, staring at clouds, jumping down the steps, jumping on the bed, pillow fights, getting "company", ribbon candy, angel hair on the Christmas tree, Jackie Gleason, white gloves, walking to church, walking to the movie theater, being tickled to death, running till you were out of breath, laughing so hard that your stomach hurt, being tired from playing. Remember that? Not stepping on a crack or you'll break your mother's back, paper chains at Christmas, silhouettes of Lincoln and Washington, the smell of paste in school and evening in Paris.

What about the girl who had the bubbly handwriting, who dotted her "is" with hearts? The Stroll, popcorn balls, and sock hops, Remember when... there were two types of sneakers for girls and boys (Keds and PF Flyer) and the only time you wore them at school was for "gym". And the girls had those ugly uniforms. When it took five minutes for the TV to warm up. When nearly everyone's Mom was at home when the kids got home from school. When nobody owned a purebred dog. When a quarter was a decent allowance. And another quarter, a huge bonus. When you'd reach into a muddy gutter for a penny. When girls neither dated nor kissed until late high school, if then. When your mom wore nylons that came in two pieces. When all of your male teachers wore neckties and female teachers had their hair done every day and wore high heels. When you got your windshield cleaned, oil checked, and gas pumped, without asking, all for free, every time. And, you didn't pay for air. And, you got trading stamps to boot! When laundry detergent had free glasses, dishes or towels hidden inside the box. When any parent could discipline any kid, or feed him or use him to carry groceries, and nobody, not even the kid, thought a thing of it. When it was considered a great privilege to be taken out to dinner at a real restaurant with your parents. When they threatened to keep kids back a grade if they failed... and did! When the worst thing you could do at school was smoke in the bathrooms, flunk a test or chew gum. And the prom was in the auditorium and we danced to an orchestra, and all the girls wore pastel gowns and boys wore suits for the first time and we stayed out all night. When a '57 Chevy was everyone's dream car... to cruise, peel out, lay rubber or watch submarine races, and people went steady and girls wore a class ring with an inch of wrapped dental floss or yarn coated with pastel frost nail polish so it would fit her finger. And no one ever asked where the car keys were 'cause they were always in the car, in the ignition, and the doors were never locked. And you got in big trouble if you accidentally locked the doors at home, since no one ever had a key.

Remember lying on your back on the grass with your friends and saying things like "That cloud looks like..."

And playing baseball with no adults to help kids with the rules of the game. Back then, baseball was not a psychological group learning experience... it was a game. Remember when stuff from the store came without safety caps and hermetic seals 'cause no one had yet tried to poison a perfect stranger.

And... with all our progress... don't you just wish, just once, you could slip back in time and savor the slower pace... and share it with the children of today?

Some can still remember Nancy Drew, The Hardy Boys, Laurel and Hardy, Howdy Doody and The Peanut Gallery, The Lone Ranger, The Shadow Knows, Nellie Belle, Roy and Dale,

Trigger and Buttermilk. As well as the sound of a reel mower on Saturday morning, and summers filled with bike rides, playing cowboy land, baseball games, bowling and visits to the pool... and eating Kool-Aid powder with sugar. When being sent to the principal's office was nothing compared to the fate that awaited a misbehaving student at home. Basically, we were in fear for our lives, but it wasn't because of drive-by shootings, drugs, gangs, etc. Our parents and grandparents were a much bigger threat! But we all survived because their love was greater than the threat.

Didn't that feel good, just to go back and say, "Yeah, I remember that!"

The following article, author unknown, sixty-one years old, was received on the Internet, and seems very true. We would be much better off if some of these customs were observed today. The deviation and some of the problems we see every day make the older generation gaze in awe.

OLDER PEOPLE ARE NOT DELUSIONAL—THE GOOD OLD DAYS ACTUALLY EXISTED

On evening a son was talking to his father about current events. He asked what he thought about the shootings at schools, the computer age, and just things in general. The dad replied, "Well, let me think a minute... I was born before television, penicillin, polio shots, frozen foods, Xerox, contact lenses, Frisbees and the pill. There was no radar, credit cards, laser beams or ball-point pens. Man had not invented pantyhose, dishwashers, clothes dryers (clothes were hung out to dry in the fresh air), electric blankets, air conditioners, and he hadn't walked on the moon. Your mom and I got married first—and then lived together. Every family had a father and a mother, and every boy over fourteen had a rifle that his dad taught him how to use and respect. And they went hunting and fishing together. Until I was twenty-five, I called every man older than me 'Sir'—and after I turned twenty-five, I still called policemen and every man with a title 'Sir'. Sundays were set aside for going to church as a family, helping those in need, and visiting with family or neighbors. (I miss that most.) We were before computer dating, dual careers, daycare centers, and group therapy. Our lives were governed by the Ten Commandments, good judgment, and common sense. We were taught to know the difference between right and wrong and to stand up and take responsibility for our actions. Serving your country was a privilege; living here was a bigger privilege. We thought fast food was what people ate during Lent. Having a meaningful relationship meant getting along with your cousins. Draft dodgers were people who closed their front doors when the evening breeze started. Time-sharing meant time the family spent together in the evenings and weekends—not purchasing condominiums. We never heard of FM radios, tape decks, CDs, electric typewriters, yogurt, or guys wearing earrings. We listened to the Big Bands, Jack Benny, and the President's speeches on our radio. And I don't ever remember any kid blowing his brains out listening to Tommy Dorsey. If you saw anything with 'Made in Japan' on it, it was junk. The term 'making out' referred to how you did on your school exam. Pizza Hut, McDonald's, and instant coffee were unheard of. We had five- and ten-cent stores where you could actually buy things for five and ten cents. Ice cream cones, phone calls, rides on a streetcar, and a Pepsi were all a nickel. And if you didn't want to splurge, you could spend your nickel on enough stamps to mail one letter and two postcards. You could buy a new Chevy Coupe for $600, but who could afford one? Too bad, because gas was eleven cents a gallon. In my day, 'grass' was mowed, 'coke' was a cold drink, 'pot' was something your mother cooked in, and 'rock music' was your grandmother's lullaby. 'Aids' were helpers in the principal's office, 'chip' means a piece of wood, 'hardware' was found in a hardware store, and 'software' wasn't even a word. And we were the last generation to actually believe that a lady needed a husband to have a baby. No wonder people call us 'old and confused' and say there is a generation gap."

This article, "Getting Old, Remembering When", came from the Internet. Ever wonder what our children and grandchildren will write on this subject:

Close your eyes... and go back... before the Internet or the MAC, before

Semi automatics and crack

Before SEGA or Super Nintendo

Way back...

I'm talking about hide and go seek at dusk.

Flashlight tag,. Staying out late on a summer evening... At least until the streetlights came on.

Sittin' on the porch, sharing a double-stick Popsicle with a friend.

Red light, Green light.

Chocolate milk, lunch tickets, penny candy in a brown paper bag.

Hopscotch, butterscotch, Chinese jump rope, jacks, kickball, and dodge ball.

Mother May I?

Red Rover and British Bulldog and Hula Hoops and Sunflower Seeds.

Jolly Ranchers, Banana Splits, Wax Lips and Mustaches.

Running through the sprinkler.

The smell of the sun and lickin' salty kips...

Wait...

Watchin' Saturday morning cartoons: Fat Albert, Road Runner, The Jackson 5, H.R. Puff-n-Stuff, Sylvester, Tweety, and Bugs.

Catching lightning bugs in a jar.

Swinging so high your stomach tickles.

When around the corner seemed far away, and going downtown seemed like going somewhere.

Bedtime, climbing trees, an ice cream cone on a warm summer night.

Chocolate or vanilla or strawberry or maybe butter pecan.

A cherry Coke from the fountain at the corner drugstore.

A million mosquito bites and sticky fingers.

Cops and robbers, sitting on the curb.

Jumping down the steps, jumping on the bed.

Pillow fights.

Running till you were out of breath.

Laughing so hard that your stomach hurt.

Being tired from playin'... Remember that?

Eating peanut butter cookie dough.

Remember when...

When nearly everyone's mom was at home when the kids got there.

When two dollars was a decent allowance.

When you'd reach into a muddy gutter for a penny.

When a penny would buy something.

When you got your windshield cleaned, oil checked, and gas pumped, without asking, for free, every time. And you didn't pay for air.

Saving Green Stamps in those little paper booklets was exciting.

When it was considered a great privilege to be taken out to dinner at a real restaurant with your parents.

When they threatened to keep kids back a grade if they failed... and did!

When being sent to the principal's office was nothing compared to the fate that awaited a misbehaving student at home.

Basically, we were in fear for our lives, but it wasn't because of drive-by shootings, drugs, gangs, etc. Our parents and grandparents were a much bigger threat! And some of us are still afraid of 'em!

Didn't that feel good just to go back and say, "Yeah, I remember that!"

I want to go back to the time when... decisions were made by Going, "Eeny-meeny-miney-mo."

Mistakes were corrected by simply exclaiming, "Do over!"

Money issues were handled by whoever was the banker in Monopoly.

Being old referred to anyone over twenty.

The net on a tennis court was the perfect height to play volleyball and rules didn't matter.

The worst thing you could catch from the opposite sex was cooties.

It was magic when dad would "remove" his thumb.

It was unbelievable that dodge ball wasn't an Olympic event.

Nobody was prettier than Mom.

Scrapes and bruises were kissed and made better.

It was a big deal to finally be tall enough to ride the "big people" rides at the amusement park.

Getting a few inches of snow was a dream come true.

Abilities were discovered because of a "double-dog-dare".

Saturday morning cartoons weren't thirty-minute ads for action figures.

MID AND LATE 1900s

"Oly-oly-oxen-free" made perfect sense.

Spinning around, getting dizzy and falling down was cause for giggles.

The worst embarrassment was being picked last for a team.

War was a card game.

Water balloons were the ultimate weapon.

Baseball cards in the spokes transformed any bike into a motorcycle.

Taking drugs meant orange-flavored chewable aspirin.

Ice cream was considered a basic food group.

Older siblings were the worst tormentors, but also the fiercest protectors.

Chapter IX

THE BEGINNING OF THE TWENTY-FIRST CENTURY

As we begin the twenty-first century, we should look back at the drastic changes and technological advances we experienced during the last century.

One of the factors that have affected our everyday living today is the workforce composition. In the early and mid-twentieth century one income was sufficient for a comfortable living. Most mothers devoted their time to raising their children. Single mothers were very sparse. Now, approximately 68 percent of mothers in traditional families work full time outside the home. They take jobs for several reasons, the main one being for extra income. It appears that now on average both husband and wife must work to achieve a medium standard of living.

Approximately 73 percent of single parents, mostly female, are employed full time, many in higher level positions where the job demands are great. This leaves the children at a day care center, or other arrangement. This loses a lot of the parental influence and attention. Other aspects are the high divorce rate (now at about 50 percent) and children being "spoiled", creating selfishness, not able to understand other people's feelings, lack of cooperation in marriages, and creating an attitude of independence and negative attitudes.

The welfare rolls of the past are being reduced by government requiring all able-bodied persons to be employed. This leaves many, with minimal education, working at lower-paying service jobs paying $6.00 to $8.00 per hour. By the time they pay social security taxes, income taxes, health insurance, transportation and other living costs, they come up short or just break even. Coincidently, the prison population's increase correlates exactly with the increase in single-parent families. There are some reports that many single mothers resort to "part-time" prostitution, or other drastic means to make money for basic means. This may be a factor in the increase of females in prison for crimes committed.

If interested, you might look into the marriage problem among only children. From information available, it appears that only children are not taught to share, are "spoiled", and have problems getting along with and communicating other people, especially their spouse. From this perspective, it is disastrous for a person from a family of two or more children or one only child to marry a person raised as an only child. The more ideal is people from two or more children to marry one also from a two or more children family. It appears that they are more compatible, cooperative, and experienced in sharing with their partner.

The student problems we experience today primarily stem from family situations, with some from peer pressure, and can only be corrected through family attention and discipline. There is a fine line between traditional discipline and child abuse. Therefore parents should seek counseling, or be required to attend parental training classes if they can't control their emotions.

Ever think of when hand letters were sent, looking forward to mail delivery, to see who we heard from today? This art is becoming lost through the advent of cell phones, long-distance rate wars, fax machines, e-mail and instant messenger services. These are taking a toll on an American tradition. One writer had the following comments:

> One day this autumn, I noticed moths fluttering insanely around a fluorescent light above my drill press and next to a shelf of dusty cardboard boxes. I imagined these moths rifling through the important documents I had stored in temporary containers for safekeeping. I couldn't remember exactly what was in those boxes, but I knew they were treasures.
>
> One by one I lifted the boxes from the highest shelf. The dust mask covering my face couldn't have possibly hidden the smile when I lifted out a bundle of letters sent by friends and family members those many years ago.
>
> It was my mother's letters that tore at my heart and lifted my spirits at the same time. Parents, take heart, the time does come

when children appreciate and remember your efforts to guide them through life the best way you can. People have a tendency to share their innermost thoughts more freely on paper than they dare with spoken words. This was the case with my mother.

I would take one of Mother's many letters, hold it in my hand and turn it over and over again. Reading a paragraph was almost more than I could take at a time. The feelings that she expressed, the love that she poured out on those pages were too powerful to digest all at once. It's funny, I didn't feel that way when I was a teenager. That was before I had children of my own, and recognized a parent's love. It is interesting how our perspective changes over the years.

"I am taking a fun class, ragtime tap dance," she wrote. I am the only grandmother in there with about fifteen others, mostly drama majors, but all fun guys. It is a hoot and I really love it. The instructor is Burchie Mann who is interesting just to be around. She is so dramatic that an old lady (eighty-two) can dance like Gregory Hines!"

In another she said, "Dad is on the mountain finally getting the last of the lambs down, I hope. They have been plagued by bad weather, there is snow there even now. I know he will be worn out and sore from spending days on his horse. The ewes still have to come down, but that won't happen for a couple of weeks."

Weekly she would to me about the goings-on of our small town. People that I haven't thought of for years came to life again in the pages she wrote.

This is why we have lost a valuable communication tool. We can renew some of these memories by saving the words your loved ones write. Write a letter to someone you love, not on letterhead, but from a writing tablet. Perhaps you could write a letter each day and mail it, but keep a copy for your journal entry. Samples of your handwriting will be appreciated later. If this method is too archaic for you, write it on a computer and print a copy for yourself (but don't leave it in the garage for the moths).

Letters are rare treasures today. Write them, ask to receive them, and value them for the historical records they are. Be sure to note a date on your letters, note the location they came from, and the address to which they will be sent. In time they will become family history over precious times.

Many of us remember when "pen pals" were developed with service members during World War II and the Korean Conflict and with students of other countries These were precious moments, when a loved one far away would anxiously await a letter from home during mail call. If you have never experienced that, it is hard to realize the joy these letters brought. Try it, you may get "hooked".

The following quotes by Paul Harvey, Andy Rooney, and the other anonymous, reflect good philosophy, and are food for thought.

A well-known commentator writes:

We tried so hard to make things better for our kids, that we made them worse. For my grandchildren, I'd like better. I'd really like for them to know about hand-me-down clothes and homemade ice cream and leftover meat loaf sandwiches. I really would.

I hope you learn humility by being humiliated, and
That you learn honesty by being cheated. I hope you
Learn to make your own bed and mow the lawn and wash
The car. And I really hope nobody gives you a brand
New car when you are sixteen. It will be good if at
Least one time you can see puppies born and your old
Dog put to sleep.
I hope you get a black eye fighting for something you
Believe in, I hope you have to share a bedroom with
Your younger brother. And it's alright if you have
To draw a line down the middle of the room, but when
He wants to crawl under the covers with you because
He's scared, I hope you let him in. When you want to see
A movie and your little brother wants to tag along, I
Hope you'll let him.
I hope you have to walk uphill to school with your
Friends and that you live in a town where you can do
It safely.
On rainy days when you have to catch a ride, I hope
You don't ask your driver to drop you two blocks away
So you won't be seen riding with someone as uncool as

Your mom.
If you want a slingshot, I hope your dad teaches you
How to make one instead of buying one. I hope you
Learn to dig in the dirt and read books. When you
Learn to use computers, I hope you also learn to add
And subtract in your head.
I hope you get teased by your friends when you have
Your first crush on a girl/boy, and when you talk back
To your mother that you learn what ivory soap tastes
Like.
May you skin your knee climbing a mountain, burn your
Hand on a stove and stick your tongue on a frozen
Flagpole. I don't care if you try beer once, but I
Hope you don't like it. And if a friend offers you
Dope or a joint, I hope you realize he is not your
Friend.
I sure hope you make time to sit on a porch with your
Grandpa and go fishing with your uncle. May you feel
Sorrow at a funeral and joy during the holidays. I
Hope your mother punishes you when you throw a
Baseball through your neighbor's window and that she
Hugs you and kisses you at Christmas time when you
Give her a plaster mold of your hand.
These things I wish for you—tough times and
Disappointment, hard work and happiness. To me, it's
The only way to appreciate life.
Written with a pen. Sealed with a kiss. I'm here for
You. And if I die before you do, I'll go to heaven
And wait for you.
Life is a journey, enjoy the ride.

I've Learned That…
by a well-known commentator

I've learned…
That the best classroom in the world is at the feet of an elderly person.
I've learned…
That when you're in love, it shows.
I've learned…
That just one person saying to me, "You've made my day!" makes my day.
I've learned…
That having a child fall asleep in your arms is one of the most peaceful
Feelings in the world.
I've learned…
That being kind is more important that being right.
I've learned…
That you should never say no to a gift from a child.
I've learned…
That I can always pray for someone when I don't have the strength to help
Him in some other way.
I've learned…
That no matter how serious your life requires you to be, everyone needs a
Friend to act goofy with.
I've learned…
That sometimes all a person needs is a hand to hold and a heart to
Understand.
I've learned…
That simple walks with my father around the block on
Summer nights when I was a child did wonders for me as
An adult.
I've learned…
That life is like a roll of toilet paper. The closer it gets to the end, the
Faster it goes.

I've learned…
That we should be glad God doesn't give us everything we ask
for.
I've learned…
That money doesn't buy class.
I've learned…
That it's those small daily happenings that make life so spectacu-
lar.
I've learned…
That under everyone's hard shell is someone who wants
To be appreciated and loved.
I've learned…
That the Lord didn't do it all in one day. What makes me think I
can?
I've learned…
That to ignore the facts does not change the facts.
I've learned…
That when you plan to get even with someone, you are
Only letting that person continue to hurt you.
I've learned…
That love, not time, heals all wounds.
I've learned…
That the easiest way for me to grow as a person is to
Surround myself with people smarter than I am.
I've learned…
That everyone you meet deserves to be greeted with a
Smile.
I've learned…
That there's nothing sweeter than sleeping with your
Babies and feeling their breath on your cheeks.
I've learned…
That no one is perfect until you fall in love with them.
I've learned…
That life is tough, but I'm tougher.
I've learned…
That opportunities are never lost; someone will take the ones you
miss.
I've learned…

That when you harbor bitterness, happiness will dock
Elsewhere.
I've learned…
That I wish I could have told my mom that I love her one more
time before she passed away.
I've learned…
That one should keep his words both soft and tender, because
tomorrow he may have to eat them.
I've learned…
That a smile is an inexpensive way to improve your looks.
I've learned…
That I can't choose how I feel, but I can choose what I can do
about it.
I've learned…
That when your newly born grandchild holds your little finger in
his little fist, that you're hooked for life.
I've learned…
That everyone wants to live on top of the mountain, but all the
happiness and growth occurs while you're climbing it.
I've learned…
That it is best to give advice in only two circumstances; when it is
requested and when it is a life-threatening situation.
I've learned…
That the less time I have to work with, the more things I get
done.

The following, "Marbles and Saturdays", author unknown, is
typical of how we enjoy the little things more as we get older.

> The older I get, the more I enjoy Saturday mornings. Perhaps it's
> the quiet solitude that comes with being the first to rise, or maybe
> it's the unbounded joy of not having to be at work. Either way,
> the first few hours of a Saturday morning are most enjoyable. A
> few weeks ago, I was shuffling toward the kitchen with a steam-
> ing cup of coffee in one hand and the morning paper in the other.
> What began as a typical Saturday morning turned into one of
> those lessons that life seems to hand you from time to time.
>
> I turned the volume up on my radio in order to listen to a
> Saturday morning talk show. I heard an older sounding chap with

a golden voice You know the kind, he sounded like he should be in the broadcasting business himself. He was talking about "a thousand marbles" to someone named "Tom".

I was intrigued and sat down to listen to what he had to say. "Well, Tom, it sure sounds like you are busy with your job. I'm sure they pay you well, but it's a shame you have to be away from home and your family so much. Hard to believe a young fellow should have to work sixty or seventy hours a week to make ends meet. Too bad you missed your daughter's dance recital. Let me tell you about something that has helped me keep a good perspective on my own priorities."

And that was when he began to explain his theory of a "thousand marbles". "You see, I sat down one day and did a little arithmetic. The average person lives about seventy-five years. I know some live more and some live less, but on the average, folks live about seventy-five years. Now then I multiplied seventy-five times fifty-two and I came up with 3,900, which is the number of Saturdays that a person has in their entire lifetime. It took me until I was fifty-five years old to think about all this in any detail, and by that time I had lived through over twenty-eight hundred Saturdays. I got to thinking that if I lived to be seventy-five, I had only about a thousand of them left to enjoy. So I went to a toy store and bought every single marble they had. I ended up having to visit three toy stores to round up 1,000 marbles. I took them home and put them inside of a large, clear plastic container right here in my workshop next to the radio. Every Saturday since then, I have taken one marble out and thrown it away. I found that by watching the marbles diminish, I focused more on the really important things in life. There is nothing like watching your time here on this earth run out to to help get your priorities straight. Now let me tell you one last thing before I sign off with you, and take my lovely wife out for breakfast. This morning, I took the very last marble out of the container. I figure if I make it until next Saturday, then God has blessed me with a little more time to be with my loved ones... It was nice to talk to you, Tom, I hope you spend more time with your loved ones, and I hope to meet you again someday. Have a good morning!"

You could hear a pin drop when he finished. Even the show's moderator didn't have anything to say for a few moments. I guess he gave us all a lot to think about. I had planned to do some work that morning, then go to the gym. Instead, I went upstairs and woke my wife up with a kiss. "C'mon honey, I'm taking you and the kids to breakfast." "What brought this on?" she asked with a smile. "Oh, nothing special," I said. "It has been a long time since we spent a Saturday together with the kids. Hey, can we stop at a toy store while we're out? I need to buy some marbles."

Don't believe those offers via e-mail that contain free offers and other "perks" that seem too good to be true. They probably are too good to be true. Here is an opinion from a friend, which summarizes it very well:

I will not get bad luck, lose my friends, or lose my mailing lists if I don't forward an e-mail. Bill Gates is *not* going to send me money, Victoria's Secret doesn't know anything about a gift certificate they're supposed to send me and Ford will not give me 50 percent discount even if I have forwarded my e-mail to more than fifty people. I will *never* receive gift certificates, coupons, or freebees from Coca Cola, Cracker Barrel, Old Navy, or anyone else if I send an e-mail to ten people. My phone will not mysteriously ring after I forward an e-mail.

There is *no such thing* as an e-mail tracking program, and I am not stupid enough to think someone will send me $100 for forwarding an e-mail to ten or more people. There is no kid with cancer through the Make A Wish program in England collecting anything. He did when he was seven years old. He is now thirty-five years old and cancer free, and *doesn't want any more postcards, calling cards* or *get well cards*.

The government does not have a bill in Congress called 901B (or whatever they named it this week) that, if passed, will enable them to charge us five cents for every e-mail sent. There will be *no* cool dancing, singing, waving, colorful flower, character, or program I will receive after I forward any e-mail. The American Red Cross will not donate fifty cents to a certain individual dying of some never-heard-of-before disease for every e-mail address I send this to. The American Red Cross *receives* donations, they don't donate.

I will not let others guilt me into sending things on to my friends for fear they will think I am not their friend… or by telling me I have no conscience or don't believe in Jesus Christ! If God wants to send me a message, I believe the bushes in my yard will burn before He picks up a PC to pass it along… But even if it comes by e-mail, He will send me one at which point I'm sure I will know it will be from Him. And if he does, I'm sure he will care enough to delete all those annoying forwards inside it.

I'm sure that no one is going to give me millions of $ if I open a bank account for him/her with money from a foreign source. They want your bank account number and other identifying information, which is either a money laundering scheme, or a scheme to empty your bank account and/or create overdraws from your account via electronic means.

Think your water supply is safe? An actual test from a water system of a southeastern city of about 65,000, a few years back, showed the following:

Hardness: actual, 7 gr—recommended, 0-1 gr

Chlorine: actual, 1-2 ppm—recommended, .5 ppm

Percip: actual, heavy/cloudy, w/petroleum—recommended, clear

Is it any wonder that people drinking this water have various ailments? This is something to think about. We wonder how many other systems have or have had similar problems. We will probably never know the whole truth.

The divorce rate in the "Bible Belt" of the U.S. is the highest, beating out Nevada as the divorce capital. Arkansas is the leader presently.

The United States has seven percent of the world population, but fifty percent of the world consumption of cocaine and other mind-altering drugs.

Our trash problem continues to get worse. Landfills are getting harder to develop. Our waterways are getting more polluted by the year, and fish from these waterways are not edible. Our oceans are becoming more polluted and commercial fishing is banned in certain areas. Much of this pollution is from hazard chemicals.

Very few families support the recycling of waste, including aluminum, paper and plastic and glass. Even state and local governments do not stress this importance.

Our water supplies are getting more polluted. Just look at the market for bottled water.

Most government officials do not represent the majority of electors, but to their own political and financial gain.

Since the 1990s, it has been acceptable to lie for personal gain, even under oath. This further deteriorates the judicial system, business, and life in general.

Our society has been so competitive and fast-track that people do not communicate very frequently and children seem to be neglected. A teacher in a class of twenty-six pupils asked, "How many of you had a set-down family dinner during the past week?" Only one female raised her hand. This may be a factor leading to children and family life deterioration. Some of us remember the adage, "Take time to smell the roses." This is still true as a majority of families do not have time for home activities. Many of us grew up, when our families had almost all family meals as a sit-down with time to discuss family issues and communication. More and more people are relying on restaurants and fast-food stores for quick "meals". This practice has led to an increasing percentage of young people obese, as well as the increasing percentage of young people having health problems, i.e., sugar diabetes, heart problems, liver problems, cancer and many other afflictions. Of course the illegal drug problem is also a contributing factor.

Technology has increased greatly. Presently anyone that doesn't use computers, cellular phones, and other electronics are almost illiterate. In the mid-1950s and 1960s a computer that used only key-punch cards consumed a complete floor of the company. Now a small hand-held computer will do more. The large computer of the 1950s and 1960s cost several million dollars. The hand-held scientific computer that accomplishes more can be purchased for twenty-five to thirty dollars. Of course with any electronic advancement, there are a few who misuse the intent of the purpose, and we must all be aware of these pitfalls.

All veteran, social, community support and fraternal organization members and officers are getting older. The younger generations are not as committed to joining these organizations and using their talent to improving society as the World War II and Korean veterans have.

Sex has been made a national pastime and recreational activity. This is a broad deterioration of the intent by God and our civilization. It is portrayed everywhere. The media, movies, and attitudes of some individuals we have elected to office, and many television "soaps" and movies use sex as their main theme. If this proliferation would stop and/or is outlawed, the national attitude should straighten up.

If you are a high-ranked employee at or above fifty years old, in any government entity, particularly military dominated, watch out. Some administrator, senior military officer will attempt to eliminate you to save costs. There is no room for educated, experienced, trained employees, and these supervisors/commanders will try anything, particularly those tactics outlined in "Management Subversion". The first attempt is to eliminate your position. For example, say you are a GS-15, police lieutenant, or similar level, some will attempt to eliminate your position and rehire at a lower level. If this fails they will resort to management subversion techniques or file some phony charges for their intent. Many senior civilian employees have heard the term "Goddamn civilian", so many times by military personnel. Especially in a military-dominated environment. The same occurs at local, state and federal government levels.

Think cellular phones are cheap or free? Think again. You sign a year contract for cellular service, get a free phone for say $25 or $30. Lose it or damage it, and you will pay $150 to $350 for a replacement. The reason, the retail price is figured in your monthly payment over a twelve-month period, depending on the amount charged or on the "free" phone.

Discrimination against sex, age, etc. has been outlawed many years ago. However, it is now still widespread. The protection for "whistleblowers" in the government was enacted several years ago. This is still not enforced, as happened during the 1992–2000 period at the federal level. The only alternative is going to court, but only two people benefit—the prosecuting attorney and the defense attorney. In the end, both the plaintiff and the accused lose in the present judicial system.

Bubble about to burst? The latest figures from the *Beige Book* reflect that personal debt is increasing to the point of exceeding their income. In 1990, personal spending was about 94 percent of income. In 2001 spending has increased to 101 percent of income. Many credit holders are "maxed out", and there is a "rash" of refinancing homes, and second mortgages to pay living expenses. Even the nation's economists cannot agree on the resulting impact on investments such as stocks and bonds. For years the U.S. has been the lowest in the world in savings.

On May 8, 2001, *The Fleecing of America* featured the U.S. Department of Education. An individual from that Department went to an auto dealer, and offered to purchase a new Corvette for $50,000.00, for cash; no questions about where he worked, his income. This Department cannot account for about 4.5 million dollars, due to sloppy bookkeeping. An outside auditor was hired to audit the Department. They gave up on the audit, because of inadequate bookkeeping. If this goes on in other areas from city/county to the federal level, literally billions cannot be accounted for.

Education has been used by politicians running for public office as a "football" to gain support among voters for the past several years.

The states that have their education budget based on real property taxes seem to have fewer problems with funds. The states that use other sources, including sales tax, and other sources have problems almost every year because of fluctuations in these sources, resulting in "proration". Every state that uses anything but property taxes for budgeting the education budget will most likely continue to have problems because of, among other changes, demographic effects. These states should re-examine their tax structure.

Many voters are reluctant to vote any new taxes because of mistrust of administrators, from the local schools to the federal level, and charges of fraud, misuse of funds, and unaccountability of funds.

Education has been eroded over several years because of promises never kept. Many schools having to eliminate some activities and courses. Many of the social problems we have today may be attributed to creating "mega schools", federal and state dictates without providing funding. The violence we have in our society today require more attention to educational needs, better family structure, and church participation. It takes all three to make a difference, and if one or two fails, the problem is not solved. The following are some ideas that could maybe alleviate the problems:

1. Require physical education classes in all grades for all who do not participate in sports. This would provide group interaction not received elsewhere.

2. Make penalties for parents who neglect their child's activities, especially on teaching gun safety, and keeping loaded guns in their household. Some schools have started teaching gun safety courses.

3. Local, city, county, state and federal agencies must put education programs on a higher priority, and rely more on local schools officials for local policies.

4. Make penalties more severe for personnel who cannot account for their expenditures, and/or cannot "keep their hand out of the till".

5. Add courses at junior high and high school level on ethics, philosophy of conduct, etc. Teach gun safety at junior high and high school levels. It may be necessary at grade school level to use local specialists, including law enforcement officers, ministers, etc.

6. Add nutritional classes at high school level. This is needed because of a growing percentage of obese children. Also, an educated nutritionist could be found in a local hospital, or other health care facility, on a part-time basis.

7. Put more vocational courses in high schools, because those who do not or cannot attend college can be ready to enter an occupation that will return them a decent living. All high school graduates will not attend college for one reason or another.

8. Some attitudes that you can't teach without a college degree must change. There are many professionals in any community who may be very capable to teach courses in their respective area of expertise.

9. Readjust the salaries of overpaid, incompetent administrators. Many comments relate to "too much fat at the top", and not enough reliance on mid and lower levels.

10. The demands on teachers are growing. We face the possibility of "burnout", teachers leaving for other professions,

and resulting in a future shortage due to not enough pay and the additional workload. This problem will not be alleviated until the government officials and top administrators "bite the bullet" instead of giving "lip service". On the other side, what would politicians have to run on if the education problems were solved.

The federal government keeps getting more into ruling our lives, and homes, dictating what we will do and where, and pass down dictates without providing funds. Evidently, lawmakers and politicians believe that the voters are all idiots. Auto safety has been getting so much attention, I expect the federal or state authorities to eventually require helmets to be worn while driving. Whatever they do people will continue to die or be seriously injured in auto accidents, and auto prices will continue to escalate due to additional safety demands.

Workers are becoming more overloaded due to cost-cutting methods. When companies reduce costs, the first reductions are quality and customer service. These are initiated by top executives who are only profit motivated to make them higher pay and increase their company stock prices on the Exchange.

It was recently reported that approximately 52 percent of workers consider themselves overloaded, resulting in long hours and forfeiture of vacation time, Thus, we face the possibility of shortages in nursing, teaching, engineering, and other professions; and degradation of service and quality of products. This also results in a higher error rate.

This overload and increasing demands on workers will most likely result in early "burnout", strokes, heart attacks and other illnesses. We have never before had so many younger people die of heart problems, cancer, and other problems experienced before in the elderly population.

Some pay structures seem to be "out of kilter". For example some college coaches are exceeding one million dollars per year plus "fringe" benefits. Other department heads are lucky to make one-tenth of that. It would be interesting to know how much in dollars the sports programs contribute to the university (or they are a liability). It appears that college sports may becoming too commercialized.

Professional sports will, most likely, eventually come to the breaking point. The millions committed to players may reach the breaking point when attendance and support abate due to a slowing economy, or demographic changes.

Many Cost of Living Adjustments (COLA) and pay raises in other areas have not kept up with the real increases in cost of living. For example, government awards COLA to social security and government employees and other areas, not necessarily on the real cost of living, but what they figure they can afford. In calculating the cost of living, all elements are not included. We never know what elements are included or not included in their survey.

The pay disparity has gotten so bad that we have difficulty in hiring prison guards, state troopers, local policemen, and sheriff deputies. In some areas prisons are overcrowded, and the population keeps growing. We pay millions per year in salaries, but we can't build enough prisons. This is another case for judicial reform, and changing the sentencing guidelines. Many inmates could be assigned to "boot camps", which would be more effective at a lower cost.

Finally, during the 1960s there was a change from the terms "we", "our" and "us" to "I", "me" and "mine". This has filtered throughout our society, including government. In other words, instead of group effort, the attitude now is that "I did it all, it was for me, and therefore it is mine".

September 11, 2001, was the worst disaster this country has ever experienced. Many functions were completely halted for two weeks, and some will never recover. The airline and associated industries will not recover for a long time. Some of the associated industries are auto rental, restaurants, motels and hotels, aircraft manufacturers, the Stock Market, and any business that depended on air travel for their business. This "trickles" down to about everything we purchase or do.

Some think that this was as a result of a letdown in our attention to what was going on in the rest of the world. It seems that, like World War II, we were unprepared for this kind of disaster. Some think it was a letdown in the CIA during the Carter

Administration, and others think that the previous Administration did not pay attention to the warnings. There have been some reports that we did not have enough intelligence analysts to process the volumes of intelligence data being received.

In any case this shows that the American people can respond together in an emergency. This is a different type of war than any we have ever experienced. The terrorist network has been found to be huge, and only time will tell what we have to do to counter this threat.

The economy is expected to improve in 2002, although there will be a "weeding out" of businesses that do not have good management, and do not pay attention to service to the dealers and customers, and customer satisfaction.

Contracting, both in government and industry, will still be a mixed bag. The honest and professional ones will grow, and others will continue to struggle. The controversy over "sole source" versus competitive contracting is increasing, mainly because of the quality of personnel writing specifications. Also the intent of the contracting agency must be defined. In other words, being open about whether sole source is justified, or if it must be competitive. If it is meant to be competitive, the requirements must be broad, in order for the bidders to be innovative, and provide their detail specification, and proposal. The sole source method may be justified, if past experience dictates, or if the vendor is the only known source for the item/system.

Since the slowing of the economy in 2001, we have all noticed the increase in various organizations using the telephone and mail to ask for donations. Most are legitimate, but some are scams. We must keep sorting out the good from the bad. One good defense is to not respond to telephone requests for donations, and carefully sort out the many mail solicitations. Remember, you cannot be forced to pay for unordered greeting cards, stamps, or any others solicitation.

The religions of the world have some serious problems. The Protestants and Catholics have been killing each other for many years. The Muslims have split and this is where the world terrorist activity is centered today. Some Protestant Churches flourish, while others struggle. The religious factions in the

Middle East have been fighting each other for centuries. The terrorist factions have recruited men from other faiths to train for terrorist activities against the United States, and these terrorist cells are located in many countries worldwide. The attacks on New York and Washington, D.C., were the worst in history. The indications were there ten or twenty years before, but the attitude was "it can't happen here", and the warnings were not heeded. These attacks changed our lives forever. They have caused a re-evaluation of our priorities, and a rededication to faiths among Christians.

What has happened to adherence to the Ten Commandments and other teachings? It appears that many Churches have not kept up with our social changes, and our educational system has faltered.

Some of these Churches only provide a history lesson in their Sunday School and sermons. They should teach how to live in our current time, with reference to Bible teachings. This would attract more of the population, and supplement the educational and family values. Churches that are flourishing use these methods. To properly mold values in children requires the Church, school, and family. A breakdown in one of these factors seriously degrades the molding of values in children.

The most serious is the growth in single-parent families, which are caused by divorce, fathers leaving and not supporting their offspring, mind-altering drugs, death, and other factors. The Church cannot substitute for the family, nor the educational facture.

We hear more and more complaints about devout Christians, unconsciously lying, cheating, etc., in their workplace or business, probably because they just do not know better. This indicates a breakdown somewhere in their teachings.

Chapter X

THE FUTURE

The future is difficult to predict. However, there will be "links" in the system that will continue to be weakened, other weakened links will become stronger, and others may stay the same. Some think that these are just "a sign of the times", but all actions are caused by people, their ideas, ways of thinking, and their environment, and situations causing their ways of thinking and doing.

Generation "Y", the children in school now, will exceed our previous generations in intelligence and accomplishments. They have greater education opportunities, will be our future leaders, with greater vision, and will develop the products that affect our lives every day. They are predicted to be similar to the World War II generation in certain aspects as described in *The Greatest Generation* by Tom Brokaw.

Unless greater emphasis is put on recycling, we haven't seen the worst of our trash problem, and alternatives for disposal. We have made great strides in packaging materials to lessen the overload of our dumpsites, but the items recyclable are the main polluters. The predictions in *The Waste Makers* by Vance Packard are still valid, and continue to be worse. The United States wastes more than many people in the world have.

The War on Terrorism will last for several years, at least, even if it can be won. Only time will tell. There are so many factors that come into play, it is impossible to envision the solution. Some think that this may be the last war, and that the world is headed for destruction. However, none of us will ever know how or when this will ever end, despite several seers and other groups predictions. The attacks this year in New York and Washington, D.C., showed that all races and religions can unite and pull together in a disaster. In any case we can expect to be fighting terrorism for many years to come.

The divorce rate in the U.S., now at about 50 percent, will climb even further as more women gain higher levels and more independence. There doesn't appear as much family devotion, dedication and cooperation in the present generation as our ancestors had. More women of today want children but not marriage. This creates a problem in our society with fatherless homes, and affects the wives in traditional homes, in seeking independence in family decision-making and maintaining family values that our ancestors had. This will continue to increase in future years, unless some crisis occurs that forces change.

Ethics now is being stressed in several businesses and manufacturing companies. However, where do employees learn ethics? Few schools teach ethics and related courses, including logic. Therefore, it is left to each individual's interpretation, which comes from the home, church, and peer attitudes. All businesses and corporations must stress these or they will suffer. Therefore the high schools and colleges must start teaching these courses, to formalize and normalize the attitudes that are formed at home, in church, and through peers. Many homes are not conducive to ethics, and the un-churched do not get this training. It appears that this area will improve in the ensuing years. Fraud and misrepresentation will continue to plague us, so it is up to the citizen to be aware of these tactics, and not fall for them on the telephone, mail or Internet. Deal with the entity that you know is reputable. Although ethics is now being stressed in approximately 90 percent of corporate America, some of the others that will continue to plague us are the recreational vehicle, mobile home, and automotive industries.

Our military will still strive to improve in equipment and personnel, although they are at the mercy of politicians who cannot understand the military purpose and way of thinking. They never hesitate to answer the call to action for the mission at hand. They deserve more and better treatment than they have received in the past several years. The Congress and Senate are made up of fewer veterans every election, so it is up to the voters to consider this in their vote. The senior military officers are at a disadvantage, because they must support the political policies of the President and Secretary of Defense.

Our education system is still struggling after several years of experimentation, and lack of resources. This will continue until the American people wake up to the fact that some way must developed for better funding, and a better method to "weed out" the undesirables. The demands will constantly become greater as technology progresses. The increase in population will also put greater demands on the educational system. We must find ways to train more engineers, scientists, teachers, and business managers. There will be an increasing demand for technicians and tradesmen. Not all students are college material, and more needs to be done for teaching the trades at high school level. Again, these problems are dependent on people, and can only be solved by people.

The entities, including government, must rely on experienced engineering opinions and decisions to advance. The ones utilizing these resources will advance, and the ones that do not will falter. Engineers are trained in several areas and should be utilized to the maximum extent in order to retain them. We will experience a shortage of these resources, if not used properly We will experience advancement in technology in the coming years, putting more workload on good engineers and technologists.

The news media at the local level are honest and good community leaders. They provide a necessary service to the community they serve, and have a good reputation. This cannot be said about the national and network news entities. Reporters "badger" government briefers, thinking they are entitled to know everything, including government classified information. This information is classified for a purpose, and release of this would jeopardize national security and damage ongoing negotiations. This security is especially critical in countering terrorism, and we must counter the demands of some of these overpaid bigots. Some would be overpaid at one-half of their current pay. Nothing will stop this until the consumer quits watching or some other drastic action is taken.

The problem of weeding out experienced, highly qualified, older employees after they attain the age of fifty, or are close to retirement, will continue to get worse unless action is taken to stop it. There have been anti-discrimination laws in effect for many years, but until enforcement is effected, and easier methods enacted to make them, it will still be almost unbearable to endure the long, difficult procedure. In other words, as in most courts, the plaintiff is the villain and the supervisor has the edge on the action, and it is a very difficult and lengthy process to endure. This type of management subversion must be stopped.

The fraud, corruption and unethical activities in business are projected to become worse as the frequency of false and misleading advertising increases. It is doubtful that it can be stopped, except if the consumer will stop purchasing from these companies. The worst are the manufactured home and recreational vehicle manufacturers, and the related finance, banking, insurance, and other related activities. In these areas, the best seem to be Fleetwood Industries, Tiffin Motor Homes, and Winnebago Industries. The others fall into various levels to the bottom of the scale in customer satisfaction.

The fraud and mismanagement in business is expected to get continually worse as more new people enter the workforce, and competition gets keener. One good prospect is the new college graduates, who are very intelligent in their chosen fields. However, unless the educational system is changed to include more subjects in the humanities, they will be lacking in this respect.

The law enforcement system will continue to suffer due to the increase in crime. They are hampered by lack of adequate pay and overload. They should spend less time on prostitution, gambling and petty thefts, and spend more time on the more serious crimes. Prostitution and gambling have been going on for centuries, and will never be completely eliminated.

The judicial system will continue to get more corrupt, unless non-lawyers stop it through more thorough investigation and conviction of those responsible. Sentencing guidelines must be changed to make them more equitable. For example, a small-time drug user should not serve more time than murderers, drug kingpins, rapists, and other vicious criminals. Also, there are continuing reports of payoffs and "kickbacks" to judges and flamboyant defense lawyers, and these must be stopped to protect the reputation of the profession and the courts.

Small businesses will survive, but many will be forced out by large conglomerates, due to deeper discounts and non-support by local, state and federal entities. The small service businesses will fare the best, although they must excel in service and attention to the customer. Government officials and our political system support what will yield them the most in both political and personal gain, and notoriety.

Every generation continues to build upon the previous generation's accomplishments in technological advancement. We will see unprecedented advancements in engineering, architecture, medical, and manufacturing technology, just to name a few. Along with those advancements, we will see more fraud, corruption, false and misleading advertising among related activities, again for political and/or personal gain We must be on alert for these negative activities.

We must be on alert for the increase in lying, cheating, murder, child neglect/abuse, and other crimes committed by religious persons and groups around the world, of all faiths. Until something happens to reverse this trend, it will continue to grow.

As mentioned before, the chain (system) is only as strong as its weakest link. No attempt will be made here to identify the weakest links, because they can change frequently, due the unpredictable environmental conditions. Some of the elements we need to stress to improve are family life/training, the educational system, and the international religions' attention to the original tenets, purposes, and methods of teaching their beliefs. Hopefully this will ease or stop terrorist activities.

Printed in the United States
863400001B

9 781931 456982